ELEVEN SHORT PLAYS

BY WILLIAM INGE

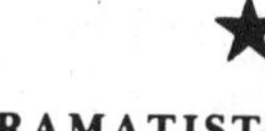

DRAMATISTS
PLAY SERVICE
INC.

 "The Mall" was first published in *Esquire,* issue of January, 1959.

SOUND EFFECTS

An audio cassette containing the sound effects which may be used in connection with the production of this play, may be obtained from Thomas J. Valentino, Inc., 151 West 46th Street, New York, N. Y. 10036.

PEOPLE IN THE WIND	Wind Bus sounds
THE BOY IN THE BASEMENT	Auto sounds
MEMORY OF SUMMER	Wind
THE RAINY AFTERNOON	Rain
THE STRAINS OF TRIUMPH	Cheering crowd

CONTENTS

TO BOBOLINK, FOR HER SPIRIT

CHARACTERS

Bobolink Bowen

Nellie

Renaldo

Fritz

Gretchen

Annamarie

Doorman

TO BOBOLINK, FOR HER SPIRIT

Every day the weather permits, a group of autograph hunters assembles outside the 21 Club in New York. The size of the group varies from day to day and seems to depend upon the number and magnitude of the movie stars reported to be inside. It is an oddly assorted group, most of them teen-agers, but sometimes middle-aged women are included. The ringleader of today's group is Bobolink Bowen, a woman probably in her early thirties, who is so fat that her body, in silhouette, would form an almost perfect circle. Bobolink has the fat woman's usual disposition, stolidly complacent and happy. Her lips usually are formed in a grin of guzzling contentment. Her hair is short and kinky; she wears thick-lensed glasses that reduce her eyes to the size of buttonholes, and her clothes by necessity are simple: a man's coat-style sweater, saddle shoes and bobbysocks and bare legs that swell at the calves like bowling pins. Nellie, a starved and eager woman in her late twenties, is Bobolink's dependable stand-by. The two young boys, Renaldo and Fritz, are friends; the two young girls, Gretchen and Annamarie, are friends also. They are people without any personal attraction they could possibly lay claim to, and so must find in others attributes they want and lack in themselves. Annamarie, in her dress, has tried to emulate one of her favorite film stars; she wears exotic sun glasses, a complicated coiffure and exciting shoes with straps, bows and platform soles. The group has been standing around for over an hour. They have learned to handle these periods of waiting like patients in a rest home; they talk idly with one another, move restlessly about in a limited space. Gretchen knits, Fritz is working a crossword puzzle. Behind them stands the doorman, a man of rigid and calculated dignity, dressed in a colorful uniform. He holds his head high and keeps it turned away from the autograph seekers as though to disclaim any association with them.

RENALDO. I heard Lana Turner was in this joint last week. Man, wouldn't that be something?

FRITZ. Just imagine walking down the street one day and . . . plop! all of a sudden there's Lana Turner . . . just outa the blue. Man, I'd drop my teeth.

NELLIE. (*Making a claim that Bobolink would be too proud to make for herself.*) Bobolink here's got Lana Turner's autograph. Haven't you, Bobby?

BOBOLINK. Lana's no better'n anyone else.

FRITZ. (*Impressed, to Bobolink.*) No foolin'? You got Lana Turner's autograph?

BOBOLINK. (*Proving it with her autograph book.*) Think I was lying to you?

FRITZ. (*To Renaldo.*) Look, Ronny, she's got it.

NELLIE. Oh, Bobolink's got 'em all.

BOBOLINK. (*She always holds her own.*) I got all of 'em that's worth gettin'.

GRETCHEN. My girl friend saw her. My girl friend goes out to California every summer. Her folks are real wealthy. She saw Lana Turner on the beach one day and she just goes up to her and says, "Hi, Lana" . . . just like that. And Lana smiles back and says, "Hi!"

BOBOLINK. Sure, she's not stuck-up. Now Katharine Hepburn's stuck-up, but Lana Turner's not at all. The best ones never are stuck-up.

FRITZ. (*Addressing the doorman, who stands with rigid dignity.*) Hey, mister, how long's Perry Como been inside? *The doorman does not respond.*)

BOBOLINK. (*To Fritz.*) Hey, don't you know anything? Those guys don't pay no attention to movie stars. They see so many of 'em they get sick of 'em. You can't find out anything from him.

FRITZ. Are we sure Perry Como's there?

BOBOLINK. (*Impatiently.*) I told you I seen him, didn't I? Well, what more do you want? I was up there on the corner waitin' for a bus. Nellie here nudges me and says, "Hey, ain't that Perry

Como goin' into the 21 Club?" And I looked and sure enough. There was a guy goin' in, had on the same kinda suit Perry Como had on last week over at the Paramount. Looked exactly like him.

FRITZ. But are you sure it was him?

BOBOLINK. Look, boy, you're never sure of anything in this world, don't you know that?

FRITZ. We been waiting here over an hour.

BOBOLINK. No one's asking you to stay. I waited outside the Stork Club three hours one night, three whole hours, and it was snowin'. Someone told me Elizabeth Taylor was inside and I wanted her autograph. It wasn't Elizabeth Taylor at all. Just some college girl trying to make out she was Elizabeth Taylor. I was sore, but what the heck!

NELLIE. Besides, you never know what's going to happen in this racket; like the time we was waitin' outside the St. Regis for Ronald Colman, and shoot! Who cares about Ronald Colman . . .

RENALDO. He's famous.

NELLIE. Not very. Anyway, we was waitin' for his autograph and . . .

BOBOLINK. (*Taking over.*) Oh, yeh, and we'd been waiting for Ronald Colman all night and we was just about to give up and go home and then what do you think happened? (*She's going to build up suspense by making them guess.*)

NELLIE. That was the best luck we ever had, wasn't it, Bobby?

BOBOLINK. Well, we was just about to give up and go home when a taxi draws up at the curb and Van Johnson and Peter Lawford get out, and we got 'em both, right there on the same spot. (*This is an impressive story. The others are a little awed.*)

GRETCHEN. No foolin'! You got Van Johnson and Peter Lawford?

BOBOLINK. (*She produces her autograph book proudly.*) And both at the same time!

NELLIE. (*Producing her own evidence.*) I got 'em, too.

BOBOLINK. See what Peter Lawford wrote? "All my love to Bobolink." I told him that was my name.

NELLIE. And he said the same thing on mine, but my name's Nellie. They're both just as cute in real life as they are in pictures, aren't they, Bobby?

BOBOLINK. Not a bit stuck-up. (*An elaborately dressed*

couple appears in the doorway coming out of the restaurant. The woman wears a dress of dramatic cut and an exotic hat. Their manner is ridiculously aloof and they make quite a thing of ignoring the autograph hounds.)

FRITZ. (*Nudging Renaldo.*) Hey, who's that? (*They all look.*)

GRETCHEN. Looks like Rosalind Russell, don't it?

BOBOLINK. Naw, that ain't Rosalind Russell. I seen Rosalind Russell. She's real tall.

ANNAMARIE. Isn't she stunning? Don't you just love that dress?

GRETCHEN. I bet that dress cost two or three hundred dollars.

ANNAMARIE. 'Course it did. Probably cost more than that. (*Bobolink is studying the woman, trying to decide who she is. The woman and her escort now stand at the curb waiting for the doorman to hail them a cab. The hounds are gaping at them.*)

FRITZ. (*Approaching the glamorous woman.*) Miss, can I have your autograph? (*The woman is a little surprised. She looks questioningly at her escort, who gives her an indulgent smile. So the woman, a little mystified, signs her name to Fritz's book. Then she and her escort disappear in a cab. Fritz studies the signature. The others flock around him to see who it is, but Bobolink is not as quickly curious as the others.*)

ALL. Who is she? Hey, let's see. It's not Rosalind Russell, is it? If I missed Rosalind Russell, I could kill myself. Let's see.

FRITZ. I'm trying to make it out. (*He attempts a pronunciation of the name.*) Irina Nechibidikoff.

BOBOLINK. (*Emphatically.*) Russian!

FRITZ. Hey, she may be someone famous.

BOBOLINK. Whoever heard of Irina Nechibidikoff?

ANNAMARIE. Maybe she's a famous dancer.

BOBOLINK. So what? She's not in the movies, is she? With a name like that.

GRETCHEN. Maybe she's a famous singer.

FRITZ. Anyway, I got her, whoever she is.

BOBOLINK. I'm waitin' here for Perry Como. I come for Perry Como, and I'm gonna stay till I *get* Perry Como.

NELLIE. (*To the others.*) Bobby always finishes up what she starts out to do.

BOBOLINK. You tell the world I do. And I'm not leavin' here without Perry Como's autograph. I been trailin' him for two

years. I got Bing Crosby; I got Frank Sinatra; I got Van Johnson and Peter Lawford and Jimmy Stewart and Tyrone Power . . .
NELLIE. Tell 'em about the time you got Tyrone Power, Bobby.
BOBOLINK. Now I mean to get Perry Como. He's not my favorite or anything, but I want to get his autograph.
NELLIE. Tyrone Power's your real favorite, isn't he, Bobolink?
BOBOLINK. (*With modest adoration.*) Yah. Tyrone's a real guy.
NELLIE. (*To the others.*) Bobbie's president of the Tyrone Power Fan Club up in Irvington. (*The others are impressed.*) Go on, Bobbie, tell 'em about Tyrone.
BOBOLINK. (*This is too sacred to be treated lightly and Bobolink is capable of dramatizing her modesty.*) No, Nellie, I don't think it's right a person should go around boasting about things like that.
NELLIE. Tell 'em, Bobby. If you don', I will. (*Bobolink, after all, can't stop her.*) Bobby's too modest about it, I think. But Tyrone Power shook her hand and told her personally that he was very indebted to her . . .
BOBOLINK. I met him at the train; don't forget that, Nellie.
NELLIE. As president of the Tyrone Power Fan Club in Irvington, she met his train at the Pennsylvania Station when he came in from Hollywood.
BOBOLINK. And I had to fight the man at the gate to let me pass.
NELLIE. That's right. She did. See, it wasn't supposed to be known that Tyrone was on that train, but the Pasadena Fan Club had wired us he was coming, so Bobby and I met him at the train to welcome him to New York, didn't we, Bobby?
BOBOLINK. We didn't want him t'arrive in town all alone.
NELLIE. 'Course not. So we went down to the station together. The man at the gate wouldn't let us through, but Bobby got by him, didn't you, Bobby? I had to stay behind, but Bobby got through and got right on the train, didn't you, Bobby?
BOBOLINK. And I hunted all through them cars till I found him. He was still packing his things and he was in a hurry.
NELLIE. But he wasn't stuck-up, was he, Bobby?
BOBOLINK. (*This is sacred to her.*) No, he wasn't stuck-up at all. I introduced myself as the president of the Irvington Fan Club, and told him we had forty-three members and met once a week to discuss his career.

NELLIE. And he was very pleased, wasn't he, Bobby?
BOBOLINK. Of course he was. And I told him us fans was awful glad he didn't marry Lana Turner 'cause, although our club don't have anything personal against Lana Turner, we never did think she was the right sort for Tyrone. And I told him that in just those words.
NELLIE. And she isn't. I mean, I like Lana Turner and I think she's awfully pretty and of course she's awful famous, but she isn't the right sort of girl for Tyrone at all.
GRETCHEN. And you got his autograph?
BOBOLINK. 'Course I got his autograph, silly. Nellie did, too. And he gave me lots of his autographs to give to other club members, but he made me promise not to give them to anyone else. (*She displays her proudest acquisition.*) Just club members. Then he told me to call him Tyrone, and he said he was very indebted to me. See what he wrote?
FRITZ. (*Reading the inscription aloud.*) "To Bobolink, for her faithful enthusiasm and spirit." Gee!
BOBOLINK. Then he had his secretary give me a picture and he autographed it, too. It just says, "With gratitude, Tyrone." Then he shook my hand and he said he wished he could come to Irvington to visit the fan club, but he was going to be terribly busy in New York, he wouldn't have a minute to spare, and then he had to get back to Hollywood to make another picture.
ANNAMARIE. (*To Nellie.*) Did you meet him?
NELLIE. No, but I saw him. He came hurrying through the gate with his coat collar turned up so no one would recognize him. I called out, "Hi, Tyrone! I'm a friend of Bobolink," but he started running.
BOBOLINK. He didn't want people to know who he was. Sometimes they get mobbed by fans and get their clothes ripped off and even get hurt. I wouldn't want anything like that to happen to Tyrone. (*Another couple appear in entrance way. The young man is dapper and handsome and the girl is pretty and expensively dressed. The haughty doorman starts hailing a cab.*)
RENALDO. Hey, who's this?
GRETCHEN. Is this Perry Como?
BOBOLINK. (*With a look.*) No, that ain't Perry Como.
NELLIE. She looks familiar, don't she? I bet she's in pictures.
BOBOLINK. (*After a moment's study.*) No, she ain't in pictures.

FRITZ. They might be somebody. They might be somebody we haven't heard about yet. (*The couple stand at the curb now. Fritz approaches them.*) Mister, can I have your autograph?
ANNAMARIE. (*To the girl.*) Are you in pictures? (*The girl smiles tolerantly and shakes her head no.*)
GRETCHEN. Go on and sign anyway, will you please?
ANNAMARIE. I bet you're both in pictures and just don't wanta admit it. C'mon and give us your autograph. (*The young man and the girl smile at each other and sign the books, while the doorman hails a cab. But this is small-time stuff for Bobolink. She has the dignity of her past career to think of. She stays back, leaning against the grill fence surrounding the club, with a look of superior calm on her face. Nellie stays by her side.*)
NELLIE. I don't think they're anyone famous, do you, Bobolink?
BOBOLINK. 'Course not. I can tell the famous ones. I can tell.
NELLIE. Sure you can, Bobby. (*The couple go off in a cab. The doorman returns to his position by the doorway. The young autograph seekers start studying the names that have been inscribed in their books.*)
BOBOLINK. They might be famous *one* day . . . I said they *might* be . . . but I don't have time to waste on people that *might* be famous.
NELLIE. 'Course not. (*They stand quietly, removed from the others now.*)
FRITZ. (*Reading his new acquisitions.*) Frederick Bischoff and Mary Milton. Who are they?
ANNAMARIE. Yah, who are they?
GRETCHEN. I bet she models. I think I seen her picture once in an ad for hair remover. Yah, that was her. I know it was. It was a picture showed her with one arm stretched over her head so you could see she didn't have no hair under her arm and was smiling real pretty.
ANNAMARIE. He's probably just a model, too. He was kinda cute, though.
BOBOLINK. (*Personally to Nellie, in appraisal of her colleagues.*) These are just kids, Nellie.
NELLIE. Yah.
FRITZ. Isn't anyone famous ever coming outa there?
RENALDO. (*To Bobolink.*) Are you sure you saw Perry Como go inside?

BOBOLINK. I said Perry Como was inside, didn't I? If you don't believe me, you don't have to.

NELLIE. Bobolink knows a lot more about these things than you kids do. She spotted Perry Como two blocks away and Bobolink don't make mistakes.

RENALDO. O.K. O.K. Don't get sore.

NELLIE. You might remember that Bobolink is president of the Tyrone Power Fan Club.

FRITZ. We wasn't doubtin' your word. C'mon, Renaldo. Let's wait.

GRETCHEN. Let's wait a little longer, Annamarie.

ANNAMARIE. I gotta get home for supper, Gretchen.

GRETCHEN. Let's wait.

FRITZ. (*To Renaldo.*) Let's wait. (*They resume their positions of patient attendance.*)

CURTAIN

PROPERTY PLOT

Personal

Knitting needles and wool (Gretchen)
Crossword puzzle and pencil (Fritz)
6 autograph books and pens (All)

PEOPLE IN THE WIND

CHARACTERS

ELMA

GRACE

GIRL

DRUNK

OLD LADY 1

OLD LADY 2

BUS DRIVER

MAN

PEOPLE IN THE WIND

The scene of the play is the corner restaurant of a small country town in Kansas. The restaurant serves also as a ticket agency and rest stop for the bus lines operating in the area. It is the last stop on the Greyhound Line from Kansas City to Wichita.

It is close to midnight and the restaurant is empty of customers. It is a dingy establishment with few modern improvements, illuminated by two naked lights hanging from the ceiling on dangling cords. Picture calendars and pretty-girl posters decorate the soiled walls. The atmosphere, like the candied doughnuts under a glass cover on the counter, is left over from yesterday.

Two young women, in uniforms that have lost their starched freshness, are employed behind the counter. Elma is a scrawny, big-eyed girl just out of high school. Grace is a more seasoned character in her thirties. A bus is expected in soon and they are checking, somewhat lackadaisically, to see that everything is ready. A tiny radio keeps them supplied with dreamy dance music while they work, and Elma likes to hum or sing the tunes she happens to know. Outside there is a strong prairie wind that sounds angry with intent to destroy. It comes and goes, creating a great blast against the windows and seeming to shake the very foundation of the frail building, and then subsiding, leaving a period of uncertain quiet.

ELMA. Listen to that wind, Grace.

GRACE. (*Unconcerned.*) Yah!

ELMA. (*Going to the entrance to look out the plate-glass window.*) It's blowing things all over the street. It always makes me feel sorta scared.

GRACE. Come back here and help me. The bus is going to be here in a minute and we gotta have things ready.

ELMA. I bet the bus'll be late tonight, with all that wind.
GRACE. Wind don't mean anything to one of those big steel busses.
ELMA. I'd hate to be riding the bus, a night like this.
GRACE. Why?
ELMA. I'd be afraid the wind'd push the bus right off the road into a ditch somewhere.
GRACE. Not one of them big *steel* busses.
ELMA. The wind's awful strong. (*Now the bus draws up before the restaurant, its great engine coming to a slow stop.*)
GRACE. (*Checking with the clock on the wall.*) Here it is, right on time. I guess the wind didn't push it into no ditch.
ELMA. Just the same, I'm glad I'm not on it tonight. I'm glad I've got my home to go to and a nice warm bed to sleep in.
GRACE. Fill some water glasses, kid. There's fresh coffee. That's about all anyone'll want. The doughnuts are left over from yesterday, but it'll be O.K. to serve 'em. Remember, we got no cheese. We got ham but no cheese.
ELMA. (*Dutifully repeating.*) No cheese! (*Now the door swings open and a young girl enters as though driven. In her early twenties, she is quite pretty in a delicate, blond way. She wears no hat and her hair is blown wild about her face. Her clothes are mainly fragments of finery from a sojourn in Kansas City, a skimpy jacket trimmed with fur, a most impractical dress of sequins and net, and gilded sandals that expose brightly enameled toenails. She lugs in a worn and beaten suitcase which she drops by the door. There is something tense in her demeanor. It takes all her strength to push the door closed again. Then she rushes breathlessly to the counter and solicits the sympathetic attention of Grace and Elma, strangers to her.*)
GIRL. There's a man on that bus. He's after me. (*Elma and Grace look at each other.*) He'll be in here in a few minutes. Is there any place I could hide?
GRACE. Well . . . there's the restroom, honey, but it's out in back.
GIRL. In back?
GRACE. This is just a country town, honey.
GIRL. Oh!
GRACE. (*Sizing up the girl.*) There's a little hotel across the way, but they'd have to get outa bed to let you in.

GIRL. I don't want to be any trouble.
ELMA. (*Intrigued.*) Is the man somebody you know?
GIRL. I never saw him before in my life. He's a cowhand from a ranch somewhere. He's been to Kansas City, riding in the big rodeo and showing cattle. He's mean and crude and . . .
GRACE. (*Flatly.*) What are you gonna have?
GIRL. Coffee, please. Lotsa cream.
ELMA. How did you meet him?
GIRL. The bus is half empty but he got on and insisted on sitting beside me. I got up and moved and he followed me. Then he followed me again.
GRACE. (*Setting a cup of coffee before her.*) Here you are, miss.
GIRL. He saw my act in the night club in Kansas City. Men are always after me.
ELMA. Do you work in a night club? (*Elma is fascinated.*)
GIRL. (*Displaying a slightly shabby pretentiousness.*) I'm a singer. I sang at a very exclusive night club there. Our patrons were some of the wealthiest people in Kansas City. I'm on my way to Hollywood now. One of my admirers is a very important man and he has arranged for me to have a screen test, so I am on my way to Hollywood.
ELMA. (*Very impressed.*) Gee!
GRACE. (*Not so impressed.*) Anything to eat?
GIRLS. No. Nothin' to eat.
ELMA. And this man is really after you?
GRACE. Get busy, Elma. (*But Elma doesn't hear her.*)
GIRL. Don't let on like I told you. He's mean. (*Now the door blows open and in walks the usual drunk, present on most every night bus. He addresses them as though they were an audience.*)
DRUNK. Just *blew* into town and gonna blow right out again. (*He considers this very funny and laughs heartily, weaving his way to the counter, dropping to a stool.*)
ELMA. (*To the girl.*) Is that him? (*The girl shakes her head no.*)
DRUNK. May I introduce myself to this charming company? I am a very learned professor . . . English literature . . . a Ph.D. from Harvard . . . oh yes! You wouldn't believe it, would you? I wrote my thesis under Kittredge. My subject was an analysis of the love element in Shakespeare's plays. I spent six years writing it. It was published in England. Oh, I am a very learned man.

GRACE. What'll it be, mister?
DRUNK. I'd like a double shot of rye, if you please, and . . .
GRACE. I'm sorry but we do not sell intoxicating beverages.
DRUNK. What a shame!
GRACE. What you need is a cup of hot coffee.
DRUNK. My good lady, I have spent a great deal of money getting into my present merry condition. It would be a sacrilege to spend ten cents *now* and start the slow, painful road to sobriety.
GRACE. I'm sorry but we do not sell intoxicating beverages.
DRUNK. You may favor me with a cold glass of Seven-Up. Yes, I'll have a rare, old bottle of Seven-Up, if you please. Your best vintage. (*Grace reaches into the cooler for the bottle. Two old ladies, obviously sister spinsters, dressed in black suits and rather Victorian hats, enter and make their way to a table. When the drunk gets his Seven-Up, he brings a pint bottle out of his pocket and spikes it.*)
OLD LADY 1. Let's not go to the counter, Myrtle.
OLD LADY 2. No, we'll take a table.
OLD LADY 1. I feel a little nauseated.
OLD LADY 2. It's the smell of that exhaust. It's sickening.
OLD LADY 1. Do you suppose they could fix me some bicarbonate of soda?
OLD LADY 2. We'll ask them. (*The two ladies sit at a table. The bus driver comes in, rubbing his hands together. He heads for the counter, addressing the waitresses in a familiar voice.*)
BUS DRIVER. Here he is, girls, your favorite bus driver.
ELMA. Hi, Bud! (*She is on her way to serve the old ladies.*)
GRACE. Did you bring this wind with you?
BUS DRIVER. No. It brought me. (*This, too, passes for humor.*)
GRACE. Aren't you the comedian!
BUS DRIVER. The bus is doing forty miles an hour, the wind is doing eighty.
GRACE. What'll it be, good-lookin'?
BUS DRIVER. *That's* my girl. Make it a ham and cheese on rye.
GRACE. Sorry, Bud, we got no cheese tonight.
BUS DRIVER. What happened? Did the mice get it?
GRACE. (*Laughing.*) Cut it out!
BUS DRIVER. O.K. Make it a ham on rye.
GRACE. Come to think of it, we got no rye, either.

DRUNK. (*Interceding.*) I can vouch for that, sir. I asked for rye myself and was refused.
BUS DRIVER. Make it a ham on *some*thing, if you're sure you got the ham.
GRACE. We got ham. (*The door swings open again, and the man comes in. He is a big man, probably nearing thirty. It is hard to say whether he is actually good-looking or whether the rugged outdoor character of his person merely gives him a semblance of good looks. He needs a shave. He wears his ranch clothes; a weathered Stetson, dungarees, cowboy boots, plus leather jacket over a flannel shirt open at the throat—clothes he has worn actively in everyday life. He stands in the doorway now, letting the wind rush in around him, till his eye finds the girl.*)
BUS DRIVER. (*Turning to shout.*) Hey, cowboy! Shut that door. (*Back to Grace.*) Guys like that one got no bringin' up. He was probably raised in a barn. (*The girl is immediately aware of her pursuer. She cowers over her coffee. Elma finds the girl's eyes for an instant to confirm that this is the man. The man meanwhile, shuts the door and moves quietly in. He can bide his time. He doesn't have to give the girl the satisfaction of knowing he is after her. He pretends to ignore her now. He moves over to the magazine rack and thumbs through one of the many lurid periodicals on display.*)
OLD LADY 2. Did you pack the presents for Melinda's children?
OLD LADY 1. They're in my suitcase.
OLD LADY 2. They'll be a year older now.
OLD LADY 1. The baby'll have his teeth.
OLD LADY 2. I wrote Melinda not to meet us. We can take a taxi to her house.
OLD LADY 1. Can we afford a taxi, Myrtle?
OLD LADY 2. We'll have to, this time of night. (*Now the man leaves the magazines and, still pretending indifference, ambles toward the counter. Grace observes a bewitched Elma, watching every move the man makes.*)
GRACE. Get busy, Elma. (*She takes a sandwich to the bus driver.*) Here you are, Bud. This all the passengers you got tonight?
BUS DRIVER. There's a few more on the bus. They wanted to sleep.

GRACE. Any trouble?
BUS DRIVER. If this onery cowboy don't mind his business, I'm gonna put him off.
GRACE. (*Meaning the girl.*) If you ask me, she's as bad as he is. She comes in here, handin' me and Elma a long sob story. It don't fool me. I got her number.
BUS DRIVER. He's just a no-account cowpoke.
GRACE. She's just a no-account somethin' else.
MAN. (*Finally finds himself beside the girl.*) Hi, baby!
GIRL. I don't believe we've met.
MAN. Oh, don't you remember me? I'm the guy sat beside you on the bus out of Kansas City.
GIRL. I still say we haven't met.
MAN. My name's Bo. What's yours? (*She only looks at him scornfully.*) I see you brought your suitcase in.
GIRL. Yes, I did.
MAN. Thought you was goin' on to Wichita.
GIRL. I changed my mind.
MAN. (*There's a deep seriousness about him.*) What'd you wanta do that for?
GIRL. I got my reasons.
MAN. Yah? Care to tell me?
GIRL. I don't wish to get off that bus in Wichita with *you*. I know exactly what'd happen. Is that clear?
MAN. What do you think would happen?
GIRL. You're strong. You'd take hold of my arm like you did on the bus, and you'd grip it tight, and you wouldn't let me go.
MAN. And you wouldn't want me to do that, huh?
GIRL. Obviously you have never associated with girls like I. I'm not accustomed to having men mistreat me. I come from a very fine family.
MAN. Yah?
GIRL. And I am an artist, a singer.
MAN. You was sweet, standin' up there before the orchestra, singing your pretty songs.
GIRL. And I told you before, I am going to Hollywood, California, to have a screen test. They want me in pictures.
MAN. Hollywood?
GIRL. Yes.
MAN. I don't believe it.

GIRL. I'm sure it doesn't matter to me whether you believe it or not.

MAN. (*With deep seriousness.*) I thought . . . for a while there . . . back on the bus . . . you kinda liked me.

GIRL. I'm sure I have no idea whatever could have given you such a mistaken impression.

MAN. Didn't you . . . like me?

GIRL. (*Frightened.*) Go way.

MAN. When we was snuggled up in the back seat . . . you cuddlin' in my arms like a little bird . . .

GIRL. (*Tormented.*) Stop it!

MAN. . . . you was so soft and sweet . . . you *kissed* me soft and sweet . . . (*He slowly takes her by the wrist and draws her to him.*)

GIRL. Don't.

MAN. Don't be scared of me, baby.

GIRL. (*Jumping up from counter, frightened, her voice high and shrill.*) Leave me alone. I'm a respectable girl. I don't wanta have anything to do with you. If you don't leave me alone, I'm going to call a policeman. (*He has not let go of her wrist. He tightens his hold on it, twisting until a little grimace of pain comes over her face and she speaks very meekly.*) Don't. You're hurting me. (*Now the man, disgusted, drops her arm, thrusts his hands into his rear pockets and ambles over to the magazines, avoiding the eyes of the others in the restaurant.*)

DRUNK. (*All other eyes in the restaurant are fast on the man and the girl and all appear apprehensive, but the drunk is too immersed in his own phantasies to pay them any attention. He begins, quite unconsciously, to quote poetry.*) "Shall I compare thee to a summer's day?/ Thou art more lovely and more temperate./ Rough winds do shake the darling buds of May,/ And summer's lease hath all too short a date: . . ." (*He has read the lines with scholarly precision plus an appreciative delicacy of feeling. The others pay no attention, they still are concerned with what is going on between the man and the girl. The man now stands at the magazine rack, his back to them all.*)

BUS DRIVER. (*To Grace.*) I *told* you. He's a bad one.

GRACE. (*With a wise smile.*) Nothin' wrong with him a few lovin' words wouldn't cure.

OLD LADY 1. Maybe the poor girl needs protection.

OLD LADY 2. If she were the right sort of young girl, she wouldn't have got mixed up with him.
GRACE. (*Who seems, for no apparent reason, to dislike the girl, says to herself or to the bus driver.*) "They want me for pictures." My foot!
DRUNK. I know all the Shakespearean sonnets by heart. I learned them when I was a lad. (*Turns to the others generously.*) Would anyone care to hear me recite? (*No attention is paid him.*)
BUS DRIVER. (*To Grace.*) He's been recitin' poetry the whole trip.
DRUNK. (*Subsides into a melancholy soliloquy.*) I'm a failure, a poor failure.
GRACE. (*To the drunk.*) Cheer up, mister. Nothin's ever as bad as it seems.
DRUNK. I'm not a college professor. I'm not any more. My students used to joke about my hangovers. One day my students picked me up off the floor and carried me home. "You are a very learned man," I was told by the powers that be. "But we consider you unfit and unable to continue in your profession."
GRACE. All you need is just to lay off the stuff, mister.
DRUNK. I've always been a very proud man. After all, a man *should* be proud, don't you agree? I loved her very much but I wasn't going to let her know she hurt me. If she didn't have the wisdom and the upbringing to realize my own innate superiority to other suitors, then who was I to humiliate and degrade myself by telling her how very much I cared?
BUS DRIVER. (*To Grace.*) Someone oughta put the old boy out of his misery.
OLD LADY 1. I do wish he'd keep quiet, don't you, Myrtle?
OLD LADY 2. A college professor! That's the kind of man we have teaching the young.
DRUNK. All I could do was keep my head *high* and leave the scene of action.
MAN. (*Has found his way back to the girl.*) What'd you have to holler out for?
GIRL. You hurt me.
MAN. I shoulda given you a beating.
GIRL. You can't talk to me like that. I won't let you.
MAN. You're a spoiled, silly little skirt.
GIRL. I'm not. I'm *not.* (*She is close to tears.*)

MAN. All you wanta listen to is a lot of sweet talk. But I got no sweet talk. (*Bringing his face next to hers, looking her square in the eyes.*) People got no sweet talk when they mean business.

GIRL. (*Awed by him.*) You sound so serious.

MAN. It's gonna be you, baby.

GIRL. You're crazy.

MAN. It's gonna be *you.*

GIRL. Sometime I'll get married—when I get out to Hollywood—to some very handsome young man in a morning coat. It'll be a big church wedding with lots of famous people as our guests, drinking champagne, giving me presents, taking my picture in a beautiful white dress . . .

MAN. Who you foolin'?

GIRL. I'm not fooling anybody.

MAN. You're foolin' yourself. That's who you're foolin'.

GIRL. You think you know so much.

MAN. (*Whispering softly in her ear.*) I'll not forget how cute you looked in that night-club place, singin' your cute songs . . .

GIRL. (*Embarrassed by the intimacy.*) Don't.

MAN. . . . and I'm not gonna forget . . . back there on the bus . . . before you got mad . . . how you kissed me . . . sweet and soft.

GIRL. I don't know what made me do it.

MAN. I ain't ever been kissed like that before.

GIRL. (*Torn between desire and confusion.*) Don't. Please go away. Lemme alone.

MAN. It's gonna be you, baby. I mean business.

GIRL. Don't. The other people are looking.

MAN. I told myself that, when I heard you singin' your little songs.

GIRL. I told you, I'm on my way to Hollywood. They want me for pictures.

MAN. (*As though she had not even spoken.*) I been a hard-workin' man all my life, since I was knee-high. I had no time for fun like other boys. It's always been serious with me, everything I ever done. I worked hard, I saved my dough, I got me the ranch . . . all mine.

GIRL. I never was on a ranch. (*She sounds very futile.*)

MAN. Now someone's gotta be there with me.

GIRL. Don't, don't. (*She is tearful.*)

MAN. It's gonna be you.

GIRL. I don't know you. You just came in the bus and sat beside me and took my hand. I never saw you before in my life. And you're rough and mean and you haven't even shaved.

MAN. (*A little smile creeps over his face.*) You don't know how *sweet* a rough, mean guy can be.

GIRL. (*Weakly.*) No . . . no . . .

MAN. Come on, baby. Finish the trip. (*He stands looking at the girl, holding her wrist. She avoids his eyes. Now the bus driver gets up and starts for the door, calling on the way.*)

BUS DRIVER. Bus headed west! Wichita, next stop! All passengers aboard!

MAN. (*To the girl.*) We'll get on another bus in Wichita. We'll be there by morning. The ranch house ain't much to look at, baby, but it will be after you get there.

GIRL. I never heard of anything so crazy.

MAN. I'll be waitin' in that back seat, baby. I'll have it all nice and warm. (*He starts.*)

GIRL. (*Getting up.*) Just a minute! (*He turns to see what she wants.*) With all this fine love talk, you seem to have overlooked one little thing; namely, the subject of gettin' a ring to put on my finger and hiring a man to tell us we're married.

MAN. (*Rather innocently.*) Sure.

GIRL. *Sure,* what?

MAN. We'll get married. What kinda guy you think I am?

GIRL. (*Truthfully.*) I don't know, mister. I honestly don't know.

MAN. (*Going out.*) I'll be waitin'. (*The girl continues to sit at the counter just looking before her somewhat dazed.*)

OLD LADY 1. (*As she and her sister make their way to the door.*) Maybe if we help with the work around the house, we can make things easier for Melinda and not get in the way. You can look after the house, Myrtle, and I'll mind the children.

OLD LADY 2. We're always welcome at Melinda's, Clara. Don't worry.

OLD LADY 1. That soda settled my stomach. (*She gives a polite little burp.*)

OLD LADY 2. I'm glad. (*They go out.*)

BUS DRIVER. (*To the girl.*) Look, miss, if that no-good cowpoke is givin' you any trouble, all you have to do is tell me and

I'll see he's taken care of. That's what the police are for, to keep guys like him in their place.

GIRL. (*Snapping.*) If I need any help, thank you, I'll ask for it.

BUS DRIVER. Suit yourself. (*Back to the door, calling out.*) All aboard, heading west! All aboard!

DRUNK. I'll spend the rest of my life riding on busses. (*Goes to door.*) Hear the wind lashing at the houses? But inside that big warm bus, you don't feel it. You're warm and snug, cuddled up in your seat, and you can coast along through the night, sleeping like a baby. With no destination. (*He goes out.*)

BUS DRIVER. See you day after tomorrow, girls.

ELMA. G'night, Bud.

GRACE. Keep the bus on the road.

BUS DRIVER. (*One final call.*) All aboard! (*He looks at the girl who doesn't respond, then goes out.*)

GRACE. (*With a little grin of insinuation, to the girl.*) Do you still want me to call the policeman, Honey?

GIRL. You can cut out the corny gags.

GRACE. If you're gonna get back on the bus, you better hurry.

GIRL. (*Standing, rearranging herself proudly.*) Who's in a hurry? Let 'em take their time.

GRACE. Them big busses, they're pretty independent. They don't wait on no one. They tell you when they're goin', then they go. And if you're not *on,* it's your hard luck. They're not gonna come back and get you. (*Now the engine of the bus rises to a roar outside. The girl hears it and shows her first sign of honest concern. She yanks her suitcase from the corner, seizes open the door and calls out.*)

GIRL. Wait a minute. I'm coming. Just a minute. (*She runs out, letting the door close behind her. Then the bus is heard going off, its motor fading in the distance. All is now quiet.*)

ELMA. Gee, sometimes I think I'd like to write a book about the people you see.

GRACE. Wipe off the counter, girl.

ELMA. Huh?

GRACE. The Topeka bus is due in forty minutes. Snap out of it.

ELMA. O.K. (*She gets busy.*)

GRACE. Remind me. Tomorrow we gotta order cheese.

CURTAIN

PROPERTY PLOT

On Stage

Lunch counter and stools
Radio
On wall:
  Clock
  Posters
  Calendars
Magazine rack
Cooler, with Seven-Up
Doughnuts, under glass cover
Water glasses
Coffee cups
Sandwiches

Off Stage

Worn suitcase (Girl)

Personal

Pint of whiskey (Drunk)

A SOCIAL EVENT

CHARACTERS

RANDY BROOKS

CAROLE MASON

MURIEL

A SOCIAL EVENT

The scene is the bedroom in the home of a young Hollywood couple, Randy Brooks and Carole Mason, who have been married only a short time and whose careers are still in the promising stage. There is abundant luxury in the room but a minimum of taste. It is late morning and both Randy and Carole are asleep, but Randy soon comes awake, reaches for a cigarette, lights it, and rubs his forehead discouragedly. Something profound is troubling him. He gets out of bed, slips a robe on and paces the floor discouragedly. Finally, he presses the buzzer on the house phone and speaks to the cook.

RANDY. (*Into house phone.*) Muriel? We're getting up now. Bring up the usual breakfast. (*He hangs up and goes into the bathroom to wash. Now Carole wakes up. She too lights a cigarette and looks troubled. Then she calls to Randy.*)
CAROLE. I hardly slept a wink all night, just thinking about it.
RANDY. (*From bathroom.*) There's nothing to do but face the fact that we're not invited.
CAROLE. Oh, there's *got* to be a way. There's *got* to be.
RANDY. (*Entering.*) But, honey, the services start at noon. It's now ten-thirty.
CAROLE. Everyone in the business will be there.
RANDY. After all, honey, there's no reason to feel slighted. We're both pretty new in pictures. It's not as though we were old-timers who had worked with Scotty.
CAROLE. Sandra and Don never worked with Scotty, either. Neither did Debby and Chris, or Anne and Mark.
RANDY. I know, honey. We've been through all this before.
CAROLE. And I may never have worked with Scotty, but I did meet him once, and he danced with me at a party. He was very nice to me, too, and said some very complimentary things. I met his wife, too. (*An after-thought.*) I didn't much like her.
RANDY. Maybe I better call Mike again. (*He picks up the telephone and dials.*)

CAROLE. What good can an agent do? We're not looking for jobs.
RANDY. He may have found some way of getting us invited.
CAROLE. I bet.
RANDY. (*Into the telephone.*) Mike Foster, please. Randy Brooks calling.
CAROLE. All the invitations are coming from Scotty's wife. Tell Mike you think there's been an oversight. Maybe he could call her and remind her that you've been referred to in all the columns as "the young Scotty Woodrow," and that Scotty's always been your idol and . . .
RANDY. (*Into the telephone.*) Mike? Randy. Look, Mike, Carole and I still haven't been invited, and I can't help wondering if there's been an oversight of some kind. After all, Carole was a great friend of Scotty's and she feels pretty hurt that she's been overlooked . . . I never knew him but everyone knows how much I've always admired him. In an interview just last week, I said "Scotty Woodrow is still the greatest." Now, I didn't *have* to say that . . . if you ask me, it showed a lot of humility on my part to say a thing like that when, after all, I've got a career of my own to consider . . . well look, try to do *some*thing, Mike. Carole and I both should be seen there . . . O.K., Mike, call us as soon as you find out. (*He hangs up.*)
CAROLE. He couldn't get us an invitation to Disneyland.
RANDY. He said just Scotty's closest friends are being invited.
CAROLE. Oh yes! Half the people going, I bet, have never met him.
RANDY. Well! What are we going to do?
CAROLE. Sandra had an entire new outfit made. Perfectly stunning. And she had the dress made so that she can have the sleeves taken out later and wear it to cocktails and supper parties. After all, black is a very smart color now.
RANDY. Did you tell Sandra and Don we weren't invited?
CAROLE. Of course not. I lied and said we were going. Now, if we don't get an invitation, I'll have to lie again and say we came down with food poisoning, or something.
RANDY. How did Anne and Mark get invited?
CAROLE. Mark played Scotty's son in a picture once.
RANDY. When? I don't remember.
CAROLE. A long time ago, before either of us came on the scene.

RANDY. (*Thinks a moment.*) That means Mark's a little older than he admits.
CAROLE. I don't know. The part was very young, practically an infant.
RANDY. Just the same, I'll bet Mark's thirty.
CAROLE. Damn! what am I going to tell Sandra? She invited us to come to her house afterwards and I accepted.
RANDY. (*A little shocked.*) She's not giving a party!
CAROLE. No. She just invited some friends to come in afterwards to have a few drinks and talk about what a great guy Scotty was, and everything. She said she thought we'd all feel terribly depressed. After all, Scotty Woodrow was practically a landmark, or something. Think of it. He's been a star for forty years.
RANDY. Yes. He was really great. It makes me very humble to think of a guy like Scotty.
CAROLE. They say flowers came from the President, and from Queen Elizabeth, and . . .
RANDY. The guest list is going to be published in every paper in the country.
CAROLE. You know, we *could* crash.
RANDY. No, honey.
CAROLE. Who'd know the difference?
RANDY. How would we feel afterwards, when we had to shake hands with Mrs. Woodrow?
CAROLE. She's probably forgotten whether she invited us or not.
RANDY. Honey, I'm *not* going to crash. That's all. I'm *not*.
CAROLE. Everyone would just take it for granted we'd been invited. I mean, we're both just as prominent as Sandra and Don, or any of the others. If you ask me, it'd be a lot better to crash than not to be seen at . . . well, you can't call it a social *affair* exactly, but it's a social *event*. Anyway, *every*one will be there. *Everyone*.
RANDY. It could be some of the others are lying about their invitations, too. You realize that, don't you?
CAROLE. (*Considers this.*) I wonder . . . well, anyway, they're all going. I *think* they got invitations.
RANDY. I don't know why the studio couldn't have managed it for us with a little pull. They should realize it's in the best inter-

ests of my career to be seen there, and my career means as much to them as it does to me.

CAROLE. Same here. Oh, I just don't know how I can face Sandra and Anne and all the others, and make them believe that we really did have food poisoning.

RANDY. You know, we could give ourselves food poisoning. Just a light case. A little rotten meat would do it. Then we'd call the doctor and . . .

CAROLE. (*Horrified.*) No! I'm not going to make myself sick.

RANDY. Just a slight case so you could tell them with a straight face . . . (*A soft tap comes at the door.*) Come in. (*Muriel, the maid, enters with a tray.*) Hi, Muriel!

MURIEL. Good morning!

CAROLE. Hi, Muriel. Put it here on the coffee table. (*Muriel does as she is told.*)

MURIEL. Miss Carole, I hope you remember I told you I'd be gone this morning.

CAROLE. Oh, yes, I'd forgotten. What time will you be back, Muriel?

MURIEL. Oh, I'll be back in time to fix dinner.

RANDY. Is this your day off, Muriel?

MURIEL. No, Mr. Randy. I'm going to Mr. Woodrow's funeral. (*There is a slight air of superiority about her now. Randy and Carole look at her with sudden surprise.*)

RANDY. Oh . . . is that right?

MURIEL. And after the funeral, Mrs. Woodrow has asked me to join the family at their home.

CAROLE. Muriel, you didn't tell me!

RANDY. Uh . . . were you a friend of Scotty's, Muriel?

MURIEL. My mother worked for him when he was starting out in the business. I was born in Mr. Woodrow's beach house, before he bought that big house up in the canyon. (*She has thus established herself as near-royalty to Randy and Carole.*)

RANDY. (*Amazed.*) Really?

MURIEL. Oh, yes. Mr. Woodrow was very good to me when I was a child. Mama worked for him until she died. I could have stayed on, but after Mr. Woodrow got married the last time, *she* hired a lot of French servants I didn't get on with, at all. But they went right on sending me Christmas cards every year.

RANDY. Uh . . . Muriel, do you have a ride to the funeral?

MURIEL. No, Mr. Brooks. Mrs. Woodrow's secretary said I could bring my family, but now that Vincent has left me and taken the car, I guess I'll have to take a taxi.
RANDY. Gee . . . that's too bad.
CAROLE. (*Thinking.*) Yes. Isn't it?
MURIEL. (*Starts for the door.*) Well, I have to be getting ready now. I got a new black dress to wear. All the big names in Hollywood will be there. I want to look my best.
RANDY. (*Holding her.*) Uh . . . Muriel, you don't want to go to the services all alone!
MURIEL. Oh, I don't mind.
CAROLE. Look, Muriel, why don't we all go together? I mean . . . well, of course, Randy and I are invited, too, but we'd be glad to go along with you . . . as your family, you know. Well, after all, you're one of us, Muriel.
MURIEL. (*Appears to examine the idea.*) All of us go together, huh?
CAROLE. Of course.
RANDY. I'll drive us all there in the Cadillac.
MURIEL. (*This idea appeals to her.*) Oh . . . that'd be nice.
CAROLE. And then after the funeral, we'll take you to the house.
MURIEL. (*Without sarcasm.*) I see.
RANDY. And you won't have to worry about coming back to fix dinner.
CAROLE. Of course not.
MURIEL. Well, it suits me. I didn't want to have to call a taxi. If you folks wanna come along, fine and dandy. You'll have to pardon me now. I have to get into my new black dress.
RANDY. We'll meet you downstairs in fifteen minutes, Muriel. (*Muriel exits. Carole and Randy both jump into action, getting their clothes out of their respective closets.*)
CAROLE. I told you we'd find a way.
RANDY. Yah. (*Taking a suit from closet.*) Say, this suit could stand a pressing. Do I have to wear black?
CAROLE. Of course, honey. After all, it's a very solemn occasion.
RANDY. Well, O.K.
CAROLE. I'll have to call Sandra. (*She picks up the telephone and dials.*)

RANDY. It's going to look all right, isn't it? I mean, our going with Muriel. After all, she's our cook.

CAROLE. Of course. You don't worry about things like that at a funeral. (*Into the telephone.*) Sandra? Carole. Darling, I'm awfully sorry but Randy and I won't be able to come to your house after the funeral . . . well, you see, we have a duty to Muriel, our cook. She's the daughter of Scotty's old housekeeper . . . yes, Scotty practically raised her. And we feel that we should take her with us, and then, of course, we'll have to go to the home afterwards. Just family and a few of his very closest friends. We can't get out of it . . . you'll forgive us, won't you, darling? . . . Oh, it's all going to be terribly sad.

RANDY. (*To himself, while dressing.*) I guess it'll look all right. After all, funerals are very democratic affairs.

CURTAIN

PROPERTY PLOT

On Stage

Beds, coffee table, etc.
Cigarettes and matches
House phone
Telephone
Suit and dress, in closets

Off stage

Breakfast tray (Muriel)

THE BOY IN THE BASEMENT

CHARACTERS

SPENCER SCRANTON

MR. SCRANTON

MRS. SCRANTON

JOKER EVANS

THE BOY IN THE BASEMENT

SCENE ONE

The setting is an old Victorian house of fussy dignity, kept in the most excellent tidiness and repair. It is in a small mining town close to Pittsburgh. Outside the house, pinned into the ground, is a small, neatly painted sign, "Rest in peace with Scranton. Mortuary." Spencer Scranton, a man nearing fifty, lives in this house with his father and mother, using the house as a funeral parlor as well as a home. Most of the action of the play takes place in the kitchen of the house—a big, clean, white room, with a table in the center. One gets the feeling that the family lives a great deal of its life here, using it as a kind of sitting room, too. At the right end of the room is a stairway leading to the second floor. At the back of the room, a doorway leading to the outside and the garage. At the left of the room, a big bay window and a door leading to the steps into the basement. A small, dark room at the left indicates the basement. It is in darkness until the action moves there. It is then dimly lighted. When the play opens, Mr. Scranton, Spencer's invalid father, is alone onstage, sitting in a big overstuffed chair in the bay window, looking out of the window through his thick-lensed glasses that blur our vision of his eyes and give him an almost inanimate appearance. He is an ancient man, close to eighty, whose life for several years now has been confined to this chair, where he sits like a discarded bridegroom, his only activity looking out of the bay window onto the little bit of world before him. After a few moments, Spencer comes up from the basement, where he has been at work. There is a troubled look on his face that one feels is there most of the time, it is the expression of a man trying to solve some problem that lies too deeply in his subconscious for him ever to see very clearly. He is a big man with long, hairy arms and big hands, yet with a kind of reluctance about him, as though his very size is an embarrassment to him. His sleeves are rolled up above his wrist, and he looks weary. He goes to the stove, finds a pot of coffee there and pours himself a cup. Then he brings his cup to his father, showing it to him. This is his way of asking his father if he wants some. His father shakes his head slowly, and Spencer takes his coffee to the table at center and sits wearily, lighting a cigarette. Now Mrs. Scranton comes down the stairway from above. She is a regal-looking woman in her early seventies, still very alert and active. This is a lovely spring afternoon, and she is dressed to go out. She looks very dignified with her white hair in a neat bun at the back of her head and wearing a simple navy-blue print dress and a small, queenly hat. She is putting on her white gloves as she comes into the kitchen and speaks to Spencer.

MRS. SCRANTON. Have you finished with poor old Mrs. Herndon?
SPENCER. Yes.
MRS. SCRANTON. Were the burns real bad?
SPENCER. One whole side of her, raw and purple.
MRS. SCRANTON. (*Makes an ugly face.*) Poor old lady. Did you fix her up to look all right?
SPENCER. Yah. Covered her face with grease paint. She looks like a chorus girl now.
MRS. SCRANTON. Son! You mustn't talk disrespectful of the dead.
SPENCER. Well, they all get to lookin' pretty much alike. One dead body after another. That's all life gets to be.
MRS. SCRANTON. The good Lord doesn't like us to complain. Well, I'm sure you've done a nice job on her. You always do. You're a regular artist in your work. Imagine—burned to death, a poor old critter like her, when her henhouse caught fire. We all have to go sometime, but I pray to the good Lord I won't have to go that way. Her family wants the most expensive funeral, you know.
SPENCER. Well, they'll get it.
MRS. SCRANTON. Is the organ tuned?
SPENCER. Yes.

MRS. SCRANTON. Elsie Featheringill is going to sing. I've got to find out what her numbers are. I hope she picks something I won't have to practice. Can the family pay?
SPENCER. I guess so.
MRS. SCRANTON. I hope so. You're going to need the money, aren't you?
SPENCER. What do ya mean by that, exactly?
MRS. SCRANTON. After last weekend in Pittsburgh. Turned out to be pretty expensive, didn't it?
SPENCER. I told you, I . . .
MRS. SCRANTON. Calling me here in the middle of the night, telling me you have to have two hundred dollars wired to you that very minute. What in God's name were you doing that you had to have two hundred dollars that very minute?
SPENCER. I told you, I . . . I had a little trouble with the car . . .
MRS. SCRANTON. You said it was something wrong with the power brakes, but they act just the same now as they did before. Besides, why did the man have to have the money that very minute? Any dependable garage would wait till morning, surely. And besides, you sounded like you'd been drinking.
SPENCER. I . . . I'd had a beer. That's all. Just one glass of beer.
MRS. SCRANTON. I still don't see what you were doing, out until three o'clock in the morning. I certainly wonder at times what goes on those weekends you spend in the city.
SPENCER. What goes on when I leave this house is *my* business.
MRS. SCRANTON. Were you with a woman?
SPENCER. No!
MRS. SCRANTON. No, you never took to women the way your brother did. Well, maybe he taught you a lesson. You see where he's ended up, don't you? A mental hospital for the rest of his life. And what sent him there? Whiskey and women. Whiskey and women.
SPENCER. (*As though it were too painful for him to think about.*) Stop it, Mom.
MRS. SCRANTON. (*With a nod at Mr. Scranton.*) It's a wonder he didn't end up the same way, but a stroke got him instead. Something was bound to get him some day.
SPENCER. A-men!
MRS. SCRANTON. Well, I've done everything I can for the men

in my family. Everything I can. If they choose to go on in their own godless ways, I can't help it. I don't know why you have to keep running into the city every weekend, but I'm not going to plague you about it any more.
SPENCER. I just gotta have a change once in a while.
MRS. SCRANTON. Lotta good the change does you. You've been jumpy and nervous ever since you got back from that last trip. Something happened there, I guess I'll never know about. Maybe the good Lord is keeping it from me, just to spare me. God knows, I've had enough to put up with in my life. Well . . . (*With a long resentful look at Mr. Scranton.*) I guess my boys didn't come by their ways from any stranger.
SPENCER. Don't pick on the Old Man any more, Mom.
MRS. SCRANTON. Who says I "pick" on him?
SPENCER. You *do.*
MRS. SCRANTON. If I hadn't picked on him once in a while, where'd we be now, I'd like to know? Did he have any ambition? No. It was me that made him go to work and earn enough money to send you to school. If it hadn't been for me, we'd be living now in a pigsty. That's the truth. You've got to admit it. (*Spencer lowers his head in recognition of the probable truth.*) Well, I'm going to my meeting now.
SPENCER. Have a good time.
MRS. SCRANTON. We ladies don't have these meetings to have a good time. We meet to accomplish things. To try to keep some semblance of order in this godless little mining town.
SPENCER. What's the meeting about this afternoon?
MRS. SCRANTON. Some of us ladies disapprove of some of the movies they've been showing down at the theater. Movies that are too insinuating for our young people to see today. We're going to see to it that these movies are not to be shown any more. We've got the churches behind us, and we're getting the businessmen behind us, too. It's no wonder our young people are making so much trouble today, if that's the kind of thing they see.
SPENCER. When'll you be back?
MRS. SCRANTON. In time to get your dinner. Good-bye, Son.
SPENCER. Good-bye, Mom.
MRS. SCRANTON. I'm going to take the Buick.
SPENCER. O.K. (*She goes to her husband's chair to speak to him.*)

MRS. SCRANTON. (*In a loud voice, for he is hard of hearing.*) I'm going now.
MR. SCRANTON. (*He cannot speak, but only makes guttural sounds.*) Uh?
MRS. SCRANTON. I said I'm going to my meeting now.
MR. SCRANTON. Uh?
MRS. SCRANTON. Well, never mind. (*She goes out the back door. Spencer continues sitting by the table, finishes his coffee, then gets up and stretches. Mr. Scranton makes a series of guttural sounds which draw Spencer to his side. Apparently Spencer understands him.*)
SPENCER. I'm sorry, Pop. There isn't any beer. Her Royal Highness won't let us keep it. (*Mr. Scranton makes a sound of annoyance.*) I'm sorry, Pop. If I bring home beer, she takes it right out of the ice box and pours it down the sink. She just won't have it lying around. (*Mr. Scranton makes another series of sounds.*) Yah. I'm sorry, too, Pop. (*Now Joker Evans bursts in through the back door. He is a delivery boy for the supermarket. He carries a large sack of groceries under his arm and sets it on the kitchen table. He is a boy of about eighteen, handsome, husky, full of quick life and humor. There seems to be a spirit of real camaraderie between him and Spencer. Spencer's face brightens immediately upon Joker's sudden entrance.*)
JOKER. (*In a voice that even stirs Mr. Scranton.*) Supermarket!
SPENCER. Well, hello, Joker, ya li'l bastard!
JOKER. Hi, Spence! Man, it's a great day outside. It's quit raining now, and it's really spring. Man, it's great to be alive, a day like this.
SPENCER. (*Laconically.*) Yah! Sure!
JOKER. A bunch of us cats are taking dates down to the river tonight. A wienie roast. Why don't you get a date, Spence, and join us?
SPENCER. (*Chuckles warmly at the foolishness of the invitation.*) Me? Go on a wienie roast with a bunch of you young punks? (*They begin boxing with each other, slapping at each other good-naturedly.*)
JOKER. Sure. Why not? You can be our chaperon. We'd promise not to do anything you wouldn't do. How's that?
SPENCER. How do you know what I'd do and what I wouldn't do?

JOKER. Jeepers! You tie one on in Pittsburgh almost every weekend, don't you? Yah, you may act respectable around here during the week, but I'll bet you really throw a ball when you get to the city.
SPENCER. Mind your business, you!
JOKER. Why don't you take me with you sometime, Spence? Huh? How 'bout it? Show me the city, too.
SPENCER. You no-good li'l bastard, I wouldn't take you to a dog fight.
JOKER. Yah? You're scared I'd steal all your women away from you, aren't ya?
SPENCER. Why, you li'l bastard, you couldn't get to first base with the women I see.
JOKER. (*With a total lack of self-consciousnss or conceit.*) Bet I could. Girls like me. (*Spencer makes a disparaging noise.*) No fool, Spence! They *do*. They really like me. Ya know why? They can't boss me. Yah! I'm real independent with 'em. I just take the attitude . . . (*He strikes a pose of boyish boastfulness.*) ho-hum, girls! Here I am. If you like me, I'll see what I can do to make you happy. Now I can't keep 'em off me.
SPENCER. You stuck-up little bastard!
JOKER. I'm *not* stuck-up. I just hold my own, that's all. And man, if you don't learn to hold your own with a girl, she can give you real misery.
SPENCER. You got yourself a girl now?
JOKER. *Do* I? Sue Carmody. Best-lookin' girl in the whole school. Jeepers, I never knew I could fall so hard. We've been goin' together about three months now. She's the greatest. A real good sport, too. Know what I mean?
SPENCER. You going to marry her?
JOKER. I sure wish I could. She wants to get married, but I just gotta get to college if I ever wanta get outa this town. If I married her now, I'd have to stay here and maybe go to work in the mines. I wouldn't like that, and in a few years we'd both be miserable. Sue was trying to hold me at first, but I had a long talk with her and helped her see things my way. She understands how it is now.
SPENCER. She going to wait for you?
JOKER. We talked all that over, too. I don't know if it's fair. By the time I get outa college, I may be in love with someone else. She may be, too. You can't tell about those things. We finally

agreed that after I go to college we no longer have any strings on each other, except when I come home for vacations. And while I'm gone, if either of us finds someone we like better, then . . . well, we'll try to understand.

SPENCER. You talked all this over together?

JOKER. Yah. It was tough to have to face it all. But I decided we'd better be grown-up about things. I didn't wanta go around feeling someone had any strings on me. Know what I mean?

SPENCER. Yah. I know what you mean.

JOKER. And she shouldn't feel I have any strings on her, either.

SPENCER. When did you decide to go to college for sure?

JOKER. Oh, the scholarship came through.

SPENCER. That's swell, Joker.

JOKER. (*A little ruefully.*) Yah, but it means I'll have to play football, and that's kind of a pain. I wanted to quit that jazz after I got outa high school, and really settle down and do some work. But if that's the only way I can get to college, O.K. I'll play football.

SPENCER. What're ya gonna study?

JOKER. Gee, I wanta go into medicine, but I don't know if I'll be able to make it. I think I can make the grades O.K. I'm pretty smart, did ya know it? Yah. I'm graduating this spring in the top five percent of the class. But I don't know if I'll have the dough. It takes about three years longer to get through medical school, and I won't be able to play football then. I'll have to manage on my own. The folks can't help me much. I might be able to get another scholarship, though. Oh well, I won't have to worry about that for a few years anyway. If I can't make it through medical school, I'll get myself a job coaching some high school football team, maybe.

SPENCER. (*Deeply serious.*) Gee, kid, I hope you can make it. It'd be great, you getting to be a doctor.

JOKER. We'd fix us up a system, Spence. I'd kill off all my patients and send 'em to *you.* (*Now they laugh again, Spencer slapping Joker on the shoulder with rough good nature.*)

SPENCER. No thanks. I got more patients now than I want.

JOKER. (*Sobering up.*) I sure don't envy you your job. I'd think it'd get kinda depressing being around dead people all the time.

SPENCER. (*Melancholy again.*) Yah. One dead body after another. That's all my life is.

JOKER. How come you never got married, Spence?
SPENCER. (*Wishing he could dodge the question.*) Oh, I . . . I just never get around to it, Joker.
JOKER. You know what? I bet in some ways you never grew up, Spence. No fool! I can have as much fun talkin' with you as with any guy my own age. And I bet you have more fun talkin' with me than you do with all the squares you meet at the Rotary Club . . .
SPENCER. That's the God's truth.
JOKER. In some ways, Spence, you're like a kid, too. Know it?
SPENCER. (*Reflectively.*) I suppose.
JOKER. (*Looking at the clock on the wall.*) Gee, I gotta beat it. I gotta finish my deliveries. (*He starts for the door as Spencer thinks of something.*)
SPENCER. Oh, just a minute, kid, before you go off in such a hurry. (*He digs a wallet out of his pocket.*)
JOKER. What is it, Spence?
SPENCER. I still owe you for washing the hearse for me last Sunday.
JOKER. Oh . . . yah. Gee, I'm glad you remembered.
SPENCER. (*Handing him a bill.*) Here!
JOKER. (*Looks at the bill and whistles.*) You mean . . . all this, Spence?
SPENCE. Sure.
JOKER. Ten bucks? For washing the carcass wagon?
SPENCER. Sure. It was a hard job, all covered with mud.
JOKER. Gee, Spence, you coulda got it done anywhere in town for three or four bucks.
SPENCER. Shut up, ya li'l bastard. If I say it's worth ten bucks, don't bicker with me.
JOKER. (*Deeply touched.*) Sure. Thanks a lot, Spence.
SPENCER. Forget it.
JOKER. I . . . I'll *never* forget it, Spence. Gee, you've always been swell to me.
SPENCER. Get outa here now before I throw you out.
JOKER. Gee, Spence, if there's anything I can ever do for you, anything at all, just let me know, huh?
SPENCER. Sure. Sure. Beat it now.
JOKER. So long, Spence. (*He runs out the back door now as Spencer begins putting away the groceries—into the refrigerator,*

the bread box, and the cupboard. He turns on the kitchen radio, too, and gets a lilting, romantic Viennese waltz that starts him whistling. Mr. Scranton utters a new series of unintelligible sounds.)

SPENCER. What's that, Pop? (*Mr. Scranton repeats the sounds.*) Her Royal Highness is bound to find out. (*Mr. Scranton makes new noises, somewhat angrily.*) Well, I guess it wouldn't hurt either of us to have a short one. (*Spencer opens the basement door and brings out a large bottle of embalming fluid, which he opens; he pours a small snifter full, which he gives to his father. Then he pours one for himself. For a moment, the atmosphere is quite merry. The old man begins nodding his head in rhythm with the waltz, and Spencer takes a dustmop from the cupboard, drapes an apron around it and uses it as a dancing partner. He is waltzing about the room when he hears the Buick drive into the garage. Then he returns the mop to the cupboard hurriedly, and puts the bottle of embalming fluid back behind the basement door.*) Her Royal Highness. She's back. (*The old man sobers up and Spencer returns to the table, lighting a cigarette and looking very solemn when she comes in. The second we see her, we know she is somehow stricken. It is as though a flash of lightning had parted the skies for a moment and given her a glimpse into some far truth she had never before quite realized, and now she is dumbfounded and horror stricken. She grasps the doorway for support. Spencer looks at her wonderingly.*) Mom, you back already?

MRS. SCRANTON. (*In a hoarse and halting voice.*) I came back as soon as I could . . . after I heard . . . certain things.

SPENCER. (*Frightened by her tone and demeanor.*) Wh . . . what'd you hear, Mom?

MRS. SCRANTON. I heard my dearest friends . . . some of the finest ladies in this town . . . talk about certain things that went on in the city . . . that made my blood chill . . . and made me understand things I never understood before . . .

SPENCER. (*Terrified but trying to conceal it.*) Wh . . . what do you mean, Mom?

MRS. SCRANTON. I was presiding over the meeting, too, and I had to beg them to pardon me. I said I had one of my migraine headaches and had to go home that instant. But I just couldn't sit there and face them any longer. I . . . I don't know how I'll ever keep my head high again, when I walk down the streets of this town.

SPENCER. (*Very flustered.*) Mom, I . . . d-don't know wh-what you're talking about.

MRS. SCRANTON. And to think . . . I raised my son, praying he'd become a great man. I raised both my sons to be great men. No one can say I didn't do my part. And *look* how destiny laughs in my face.

SPENCER. Mom, t-tell me.

MRS. SCRANTON. (*Spying the book of matches on the kitchen table which Spencer has been using to light cigarettes. She grabs them and forces them in his face.*) Where did you get these matches? (*Her very tone is like a condemnation to hell.*)

SPENCER. I . . . uh . . . I don't remember, Mom. I g-guess I just picked them up some place.

MRS. SCRANTON. The Hi Ho Bar . . . in Pittsburgh. That's where they came from.

SPENCER. Yah, I see, Mom. I . . . I don't know *where* I got 'em.

MRS. SCRANTON. You got them when you went there last Saturday night, and the place was raided, and you called me for two hundred dollars to pay the policeman to keep him from putting you in jail and to keep your name out of the paper. (*Her detective work has thoroughly shattered Spencer's nerves. He can no longer look at her. He cannot even speak. His incoherent grunts give him a moment's resemblance to his father's mumbling inarticulateness.*) And the police raided the place because it's a meeting place for degenerates. (*Spencer collapses over the table, his head in his arms. Mrs. Scranton now has the bearing of a tragic victor.*) Dear God, my own son! My own flesh and blood! Corrupting himself in low degeneracy. Going to some disgusting saloon, where men meet other men and join together in . . . in some form of unnatural vice, in some form of . . . of lewd depravity. (*With this, Spencer runs upstairs in panic. Mrs. Scranton now drops to the floor, on her knees, leaning on the table in anguished prayer.*) O God, why do you make me suffer so? Why do you thrust every kind of sorrow and humiliation on me to endure? Haven't I always tried to live in your holy light? And haven't I always fought to keep my family there? My loved ones? Why do you continue to punish me, O Lord? I've loved my son since the day he was born and kept him to my breast with loving care. I think I even loved him more than I loved my own husband, for my son's infant love was innocent and pure, and demanded no fleshly act to satisfy its need. O God, will you punish me forever? *I*, who have fought so hard for the *right!* Have fought so hard to keep my mind and heart and body *pure* and free from all physical craving. All my life, I've been a God-fearing woman. Maybe you punish me for sins I don't know anything about. Are you, O Lord? Are you punishing me for sins I know not of? Then tell me, so I can atone for them and be forgiven. I don't want to suffer all my life long. When was the day I did wrong? Dear God, when was the day I did wrong? (*Spencer comes hurrying down the stairs now, wearing the jacket to his conservative blue suit, a white shirt, a dark tie and a gray hat. He carries a topcoat over one arm and a suitcase. He has made up his mind what he has to do. He heads straight for the back door, Mrs. Scranton slowly rousing herself to the fact of his leaving.*) Son! Where you going?

SPENCER. I don't know. I'm just goin'.

MRS. SCRANTON. (*Getting up, running to him and grasping his arm.*) Son!

SPENCER. I should have left here a long time ago, but I didn't. I just stayed on, and on, and on. But I'm going now. Never you fear. And it'll be a cold day in hell before I ever come back.

MRS. SCRANTON. Son! Listen to me. Now don't do anything crazy . . .

SPENCER. I suppose it's something crazy if I wanta be my own boss. Forty-six years old. And I stay around here and listen to your yapping. I don't have to do it. See? I'm as free as the next one. I can get a job like that. (*Snaps his fingers.*) And live the way I wanta live. And to hell with you!

MRS. SCRANTON. (*Breathlessly.*) I'm your mother, Son. I'm your mother. You can't leave your old home. Now think a minute . . .

SPENCER. (*Loosening her hands on his arm.*) It's no use, Mom. I'm goin'. By God, I'm goin'. (*He tears out the door.*)

MRS. SCRANTON. (*Crying desperately.*) Son! Son! Don't do anything foolish. Come back here, Son. You'll be sorry you left this way. Now come back here and be reasonable. (*But she only hears the sound of the Buick pull out of the garage and drive away. She utters one last futile cry.)* Son! *(But he is gone. She drags herself back into the kitchen and drops into the chair by the table.)* Oh God, give me peace! Give me peace! *(She sobs. Mr. Scranton has not moved throughout the scene but has continued staring out the window like a piece of patient wreckage.)*

CURTAIN

SCENE TWO

It is early the next morning. The sun just beginning to show and bring a soft light to the interior of the house. Mrs. Scranton is alone onstage, sitting in her husband's chair, looking out of the window but seeing nothing. She is dressed in a long night dress and loose robe, her long, white hair down her back. Her face is stricken with emptiness and grief. She is absolutely immobile for several moments. Then she hears the Buick drive into the driveway, into the garage. A wave of relief comes over her that makes us think for a moment she might faint. But she has never fainted in her life, and she doesn't now. In a few moments Spencer comes in carrying his suitcase, tossing his hat on the post at the bottom of the stairway. He is defeated and knows it. And his bearing tells us he accepts the fact, although sadly. He sets the suitcase down at the bottom of the stairs and stands there, not knowing what to say, hoping his mother will take over the situation. But she doesn't. There is something almost shy about the woman now, and her eyes are full and her chin trembles. Finally, Spencer speaks.

SPENCER. That you, Mom?
MRS. SCRANTON. *(Jumps up from her chair and runs to him.)* My boy! My boy! My boy! *(All the fears and resentments they have fought inside themselves during the past several hours are purged now in a fast embrace. Their need, their desperate dependence on each other, their deep love bring them together like lovers.)*

SPENCER. Mom! (*They share a fast embrace. Undoubtedly, this is the only person Spencer truly loves.*)
MRS. SCRANTON. Oh, my son! Thank God you're back. If you hadn't come back, I'd have been ready for the basement myself.
SPENCER. Yah. I came back.
MRS. SCRANTON. You won't ever leave me again, will you, Son?
SPENCER. No, Mom.
MRS. SCRANTON. Because it's like we'd made a pact together, a long time ago. If one of us breaks it, we're both destroyed.
SPENCER. I know it, Mom.
MRS. SCRANTON. I've just been sitting here all night. I got your father to bed and then came down here and just sat, staring out the window. It's morning now, isn't it? Where have you been, Son?
SPENCER. I just drove all over, one town to another. Not stopping any place. Just driving. I'm not sure I know now where I've been.
MRS. SCRANTON. Well, you're back now. That's the important thing. And we're going to try to treat each other nicer now, aren't we? To speak to each other with a little more consideration.
SPENCER. Sure, Mom.
MRS. SCRANTON. It's just all wrong for us to get so impatient with each other.
SPENCER. Sure, Mom.
MRS. SCRANTON. (*Sighing deeply.*) Oh, God, I'm still heaving with relief. (*Upstairs now, Mr. Scranton makes some guttural noises that demand their attention.*) Your father's up. You go help him downstairs and I'll get your breakfast. (*Now there is a knocking at the back door.*) Oh, it's the body. I took a call for you while you were gone. Some young boy got drowned in the river last night. They said they'd bring the body over first thing this morning. I was too distracted to get the details.
SPENCER. One dead body after another. That's all my life is.
MRS. SCRANTON. Now, Son, let's not complain.
SPENCER. How'd you know I'd be back?
MRS. SCRANTON. (*A little hesitantly, with just an edge of guilt.*) I . . . I thought . . . you would be. (*Spencer accepts*

the minor debasement and her self-confidence, and goes wearily upstairs as Mrs. Scranton opens the back door, admitting two men, dressed as miners, carrying a body on a stretcher, the body covered with a blanket.) Right this way, gentlemen. Over here to the basement door. (*The two silent men carry the body through the kitchen to the basement door, then down the stairs, as Spencer brings his father down the stairs from the second floor, the old man hanging onto Spencer with infant dependence, having to feel his way cautiously every step he takes. Down in the basement, the two men put the body on a long white slab, something like a kitchen sideboard, that drains into a big sink. They keep their heads down in heavy grief. Mrs. Scranton is talking with them in a low voice that comes over to the audience as just a mumble. Their answers to her are monosyllables. She is a business woman now. Spencer is just getting his father into the big chair as Mrs. Scranton leads the two men up from the basement.*) Yes, we'll take care of the dear boy. My son does the best work in town. You can ask anyone. I know what a grief it is to you, sudden death always is. But he'll have the boy looking like he could sit up and speak to you. He'll have a fine Christian burial. You may depend on that. (*She lets the two men out the back door now, and turns to Spencer.*) It's the Evans boy. (*Spencer gasps.*) Delivered groceries here for the supermarket. The one that washed your hearse for you sometimes.

SPENCER. (*As though to himself.*) No . . . no . . .

MRS. SCRANTON. (*Busying herself at the stove, getting breakfast.*) The little fool, he and a bunch of kids decided to go swimming last night in the river. Boys and girls together, going in swimming *naked*. Oh! That's what they do. Those high school kids have no shame. What are things coming to? And after all these spring rains. They might have known what to expect. Oh, that old devil river gets someone every year.

SPENCER. (*Runs down the basement stairs.*) Joker! Joker! (*He tears the blanket off the young, naked body and stares at it, unable to believe what has happened. Then he returns slowly back up the stairs to the kitchen.*) Mom! It's Joker! It's Joker!

MRS. SCRANTON. I know. That's what I was trying to tell you. The little fool went in swimming after all these spring rains we've been having. Should have known better. Oh, that old devil river gets someone every year.

SPENCER. (*Can only mutter to himself with a feeling of mysterious loss.*) Joker! Joker!
MRS. SCRANTON. I'm afraid you'll have to get right to work on him. They want the funeral tomorrow. They just want the cheap funeral, too, so don't go to any extra pains. Remember, you've got old Mrs. Herndon's funeral this afternoon at two-thirty. I've got to practice some of Elsie Featheringill's numbers, too. (*Dazed, Spencer returns to the basement and stands beside the body, just staring at it. Mrs. Scranton goes over to her husband's chair and delivers an ultimatum.*) There'll be no more whiskey drinking.
MR. SCRANTON. Uh?
MRS. SCRANTON. (*Louder.*) I said there'll be no more whiskey drinking. I found where you were hiding it, in the bottle of embalming fluid.
MR. SCRANTON. Uh?
MRS. SCRANTON. Nothing! How do you want your eggs?
MR. SCRANTON. Uh?
MRS. SCRANTON. I said, how do you want your eggs?
MR. SCRANTON. Uh?
MRS. SCRANTON. (*Giving up.*) Well, I'll poach them. They're easier on the digestion.
MR. SCRANTON. Uh?
MRS. SCRANTON. (*Shouting.*) Nothing! (*To herself now, returning to stove.*) You don't *want* to hear me. You never did want to hear me. I could holler my lungs out and you still wouldn't hear me. (*She is busy getting breakfast. Mr. Scranton looks out of his window on a sunny morning, birds twittering now in the trees. Mrs. Scranton, contented as a new bride, sings "Rock of Ages" as she gets breakfast. Down in the basement, Spencer finally moves from his frozen stance at Joker's side to rub one soft hand warmly over the boy's chest, as though it were precious metal.*)
SPENCER. (*In a tone of reverence and awe.*) Joker, you little bastard! I never expected to see you down here. Why couldn't you have been more careful, boy? You were alive. Didn't you appreciate it? Most of us are just pretending, and it don't matter when we end up down here. But you were alive. You were alive. Jesus! And I wanted you to stay that way. (*Mrs. Scranton, a lit-*

tle curious as to what is going on, sticks her head in the basement door and calls down.)

MRS. SCRANTON. (*Suspiciously.*) What are you doing down there?

SPENCER. You'd be suspicious if I was in the same room with a stuffed owl.

MRS. SCRANTON. Don't be sassy. (*Spencer has no retort.*) You can eat your breakfast while he's draining, can't you?

SPENCER. (*In a firm voice.*) I won't want any breakfast.

MRS. SCRANTON. Oh, well you'll want coffee. It's ready. Do you want me to help you down there?

SPENCER. (*Most definitely.*) I do *not.*

MRS. SCRANTON. Well, you don't have to bite my head off. (*She slams the door and goes back to her work. Spencer now picks up one of the boy's hands and kisses it warmly.*)

SPENCER. Jesus Christ, Joker, I wanted you to live. (*Now he takes his scalpel. It is the hardest thing he ever had to do in his life, and he has to steel himself to do it, but he severs the main arteries, feeling the pain of doing it to himself, and then drops to a chair, his perspiring face in his hands.*)

CURTAIN

PROPERTY PLOT

On Stage

Cupboard, with dust mop and apron
Refrigerator
Bread box
Kitchen table and chairs
Matches, on table
Overstuffed chair
Stove, with pot of coffee
Coffee cups
Glasses
Radio
Clock, on wall
White slab and sink
Scalpel

Off Stage

Sack of groceries (Joker)
Bottle of "embalming fluid"
Suitcase (Spencer)
"Body" on stretcher, with blanket

Personal

Cigarettes } (Spencer)
Wallet, with bills }

THE TINY CLOSET

CHARACTERS

Mr. Newbold

Mrs. Crosby

Elsie

Mrs. Hergesheimer

THE TINY CLOSET

The scene is a boarding-rooming house somewhere in a Midwestern city. On stage we see the big living room of the house, which is Victorian in design, with ornate woodwork and high ceiling. The furnishings, too, are Victorian. An ornate wooden stairway is at the right, and the outside entrance is down right. As the curtain goes up, Mr. Newbold is seen coming down the stairs. He is a man of about fifty, a large man and rather nice-looking. He is always impeccably dressed in the most conservative clothes, a dark blue suit, white shirt, modest tie, a high shine on his black shoes, and his thinning hair carefully combed. He is the sort of man who takes great pride in his grooming. Something now seems to be bothering him. When he gets to the bottom of the stairs, he stops a moment and thinks. Then he calls his landlady.

MR. NEWBOLD. Mrs. Crosby! (*No response.*) Mrs. Crosby!
MRS. CROSBY. (*Coming from the kitchen.*) Yes, Mr. Newbold. I was just straightening up after breakfast. I'm afraid none of the guests like the new bacon I got. It's just as expensive as the other bacon I was serving. On my word it is. Every bit. I didn't buy it to bring down expenses. Not at all. It's *fine bacon.* Hickory smoked. Only it's the kind you slice yourself. That's why I got it. You can cut yourself a good thick slice of bacon that you can really get your teeth into, instead of that other stuff that shrivels up like tissue paper . . . (*She is the sort of woman who continues talking until someone stops her.*)
MR. NEWBOLD. Mrs. Crosby . . .
MRS. CROSBY. Yes, Mr. Newbold!
MR. NEWBOLD. Mrs. Crosby, you remember before I moved in I specified that no one was to enter my closet . . .
MRS. CROSBY. Indeed I remember, Mr. Newbold. And I told you you could have your own lock on the closet, like you asked me. No one around here has any keys to your closet but *you,* Mr. Newbold . . .

MR. NEWBOLD. Nevertheless, Mrs. Crosby . . .
MRS. CROSBY. . . . and I told the colored woman, "Elsie, you're not to enter Mr. Newbold's closet. Mr. Newbold," I told her, "is a perfectly orderly gentleman who is perfectly capable of keeping his own closet, and you're not to bother it." I gave her strict orders, Mr. Newbold.
MR. NEWBOLD. Nevertheless, Mrs. Crosby . . .
MRS. CROSBY. And as for me, goodness, I never go near the rooms. I got enough on my hands downstairs without bothering about the upstairs. I leave all that to Elsie. I don't suppose I been upstairs now in almost . . .
MR. NEWBOLD. Mrs. Crosby, a closet is a very small space. That's all I ask in this life. That's all I ask, just that tiny closet to call my own, my very own.
MRS. CROSBY. I quite understand, Mr. Newbold. We all have to have some place that's private to us, where we don't invite the world to see. I quite understand.
MR. NEWBOLD. But someone has been monkeying with the lock on the door, Mrs. Crosby.
MRS. CROSBY. (*Shocked.*) You don't say!
MR. NEWBOLD. I *do* say, Mrs. Crosby. Someone has been monkeying with that expensive Yale lock I had put on the door.
MRS. CROSBY. Do you suppose someone coulda got up there when no one was around and . . .
MR. NEWBOLD. I'm sure I don't know, but I won't stand for anyone's monkeying with that lock, Mrs. Crosby. That room, while I rent it, is my private property, and I gave strict instructions that no one was to go near the closet, and I expect my orders to be respected.
MRS. CROSBY. Of course, Mr. Newbold, you're my favorite of all the roomers. Oh, I wish they was all like you. You keep your room spotless, and you're always so correct around the house. My, you're a model guest. You really are. You should open up a class out here at that night school they have for adults and teach 'em how to behave in their rooming houses. The landladies in this town would get together and thank you.
MR. NEWBOLD. Thank you, Mrs. Crosby. Nevertheless, I must repeat that that closet is my personal property. There is nothing inside I am ashamed of. It's not that. It's only that I have *some*

place, just some little place, that's completely private. That no one has access to. That's all I ask, Mrs. Crosby.
MRS. CROSBY. And I quite understand, Mr. Newbold.
MR. NEWBOLD. Very well. As long as that is clearly understood, I hope I'll not have to bring the subject up again, Mrs. Crosby.
MRS. CROSBY. I'll tell Elsie again, Mr. Newbold. I'll give special emphasis that no one is to go near that closet.
MR. NEWBOLD. Thank you, Mrs. Crosby. (*Looks at his watch.*) Goodness! I mustn't dally another minute.
MRS. CROSBY. Did you see Mrs. Hergesheimer in the store yesterday, Mr. Newbold?
MR. NEWBOLD. Mrs. Hergesheimer? Oh, yes, I believe I did.
MRS. CROSBY. She called me yesterday and told me she seen you. "Whata fine man that Mr. Newbold is!" she says. "You're a lucky woman, Mrs. Crosby, to have such a fine guest. All I got in my home is a lota old-maid school teachers and I'm always cleanin' up after 'em." That's what she says. "Oh, men are much tidier than women, I told her." I kept school teachers once and they was always in the bathroom, curling their hair in there or giving themselves shampoos, or shaving their legs on my nice bedspreads. *Mr.* Crosby was alive then, and it almost drove him crazy. He never could get to the bathroom when he wanted to, because of them school teachers.
MR. NEWBOLD. Good day, Mrs. Crosby. (*He puts on his hat and goes out the door.*)
MRS. CROSBY. Good day, Mr. Newbold! (*Calling to him outside the door.*) You be here for dinner tonight, won't you?
MR. NEWBOLD. (*Off.*) I intend to be.
MRS. CROSBY. (*Closing the door.*) Good day, Mr. Newbold. (*Now she comes back inside the room. Curiosity is about to kill her. She is childishly excited. She goes back to the door and peers out to make sure that Mr. Newbold is on his way. Then she comes back and goes to the telephone, dialing her number.*) Mrs. Hergesheimer? Have you got a minute? He's just left. "You're not to go into my room," he says to me again, for the two-hundredth time. "Someone's been playing with the lock on my door and you're not to go near that closet," he says, like it was his house and he was ordering me about. Can you beat it? Now what do you suppose he's got hid away in that closet? (*She lis-*

tens awhile.) No, I can't think he'd be a Communist, Mrs. Hergesheimer. Of course, he *might* be. You never can tell. But I don't think that's it, somehow. (*She listens again.*) Love letters? But why would he need a whole closet for his love letters, if he's got any. Besides, I don't think he's the type of man that has love letters. (*She listens.*) It's certainly a mystery. I confess, it's certainly a mystery. What would *you* do, Mrs. Hergesheimer? (*A pause.*) You would? Well, hurry over, why don't you, and we'll try again. Hurry! (*She hangs up, then calls to the kitchen.*) Elsie, you're not to go upstairs for a while. Mrs. Hergesheimer is comin' over and she and I have some things we wanta do up there, so you're to keep busy with the washin'. Understand?

ELSIE. (*Off.*) Yes, Mrs. Crosby. (*Now Mrs. Crosby spends a few minutes of nervous activity. Her conscience bothers her some, but primarily she is afraid of being caught. She looks out the door again, then out of each window, then calls out to the kitchen again.*)

MRS. CROSBY. Remember, Elsie, you're not to bother me for a while. I'll let you know when I want you, Elsie. You're to stay out there till I call you. (*Now Mrs. Hergesheimer hurries into the house.*)

MRS. HERGESHEIMER. I think you've got every *right*, Mrs. Crosby. Every right.

MRS. CROSBY. That's what I've been telling myself, Mrs. Hergesheimer. I've got every *right*. For all I know, I may be harboring a *spy*, or a criminal, or a lunatic. What's he got in that closet that he don't want anyone to see? Can you tell me? It must be something he's ashamed of, or he wouldn't mind if anyone saw. Isn't that what you say? And if it's something he's ashamed of, I think we should find out what it is. You can't tell, he might have a bomb in there he meant to destroy us with. I'm not gonna set idly by while someone is plotting something, Mrs. Hergesheimer. I pride myself, I'm a real American, and I say, if anyone's got any secrets he wants to keep hid, let 'em come out into the open and declare himself. Mr. Newbold has always seemed like a fine man, and I got nothin' against him personally, and he's the best roomer I ever had, keeps his room spotless. Elsie don't have to do anything but make the bed. And I appreciate that, but it you ask me, it's kinda unnatural for a man to be so tidy. Isn't that what you say? There's been something suspicious about him from the very first.

MRS. HERGESHEIMER. I made a point of talking to him when I was shopping in Baumgarden's yesterday. My, he struts around that floor. You'd think he was president instead of a floorwalker. I asked him where they kept the artificial flowers. I knew, but I just wanted to see if he'd recognize me. He smiled and made a lordly gesture with his hand, showin' me the way. You'd have thought he was the King of Persia with all his fine manners.

MRS. CROSBY. He belongs to the Lions' Club. Do you think he'd be a Communist and still belong to the Lions' Club?

MRS. HERGESHEIMER. You can't tell. Lots of them join clubs like that just as a cover-up. That school teacher I got—she's a Red and I know it. Brings home all kinds of books to read. Yes. Dangerous books. But she goes to church every Sunday morning, just as big as you please, just to pretend she's *not* a Red..

MRS. CROSBY. Forevermore!

MRS. HERGESHEIMER. I think you've got every right to go into that closet, Mrs. Crosby.

MRS. CROSBY. Yes, I think so, too. Well . . . well, you come with me.

MRS. HERGESHEIMER. Oh, Mrs. Crosby, honey, I don't think it's right for me to do it. I'll stay down here and see that Elsie doesn't bother you.

MRS. CROSBY. I'm not going to do it if you don't come with me.

MRS. HERGESHEIMER. Well . . .

MRS. CROSBY. After all, you've been just as curious about this as I've been, and I think you owe it to me to come along.

MRS. HERGESHEIMER. Well, if that's the way you feel about it, Mrs. Crosby, I'll come along. After all, it's not as though we were doing anything criminal.

MRS. CROSBY. Indeed it's not. Come on then. (*She starts toward the stairs, taking a final look toward the kitchen to make sure that Elsie is occupied.*)

MRS. HERGESHEIMER. (*Following with some trepidation.*) Oh dear, I hope he doesn't find out.

MRS. CROSBY. We can get that lock off this time without making any more scratches than we made yesterday. He won't notice.

MRS. HERGESHEIMER. Oh, I bet he does. He's got a sharp eye.

MRS. CROSBY. Well, I don't care if he does. I've got a right to see what's in that closet.
MRS. HERGESHEIMER. Yes . . . Well . . . go on, Mrs. Crosby. I'm right behind you. (*Slowly, cautiously, the two women go up the stairs together. The stage is empty for a few moments, then Elsie comes in from the kitchen, looks up the stairs with curiosity. Then, as though the behavior of the two women was too much for her to understand, she shrugs her shoulders, laughs gently, and returns to kitchen. The stage is empty again for a few moments. Then, slowly, the front door opens and Mr. Newbold returns inside the house. He has suspected the two women to do exactly what they're doing. He is very nervous. His heart is pounding. He starts up the stairs and then comes down again. He can't seem to get the courage to confront the women. The starch he showed earlier in the play has dissolved. He is perspiring heavily and twisting his hands in fear and excitement. In a few moments we hear the women on their way downstairs. Mr. Newbold hurriedly finds a closet to hide in. The two women come down the stairs slowly, in awed silence. Mrs. Crosby carries a woman's hat, a large hat, the kind a graceful lady might wear to a garden party. It 's quite a lovely hat, in a light pastel color with great flowers on its limber brim and sleek satin ribbons. They come forward together, Mrs. Crosby holding the hat, both of them studying it with bafflement.*) Hats! Dozens of hats!
MRS. CROSBY. I can't believe it.
MRS. HERGESHEIMER. He must have brought them home from the store, don't you think?
MRS. CROSBY. But there was all that sewing equipment on a shelf.
MRS. HERGESHEIMER. But no man could make hats as lovely as these.
MRS. CROSBY. I don't know. There's something kinda unusual about Mr. Newbold. I think he might have made them. I . . . I know he did. (*Suddenly recalls a clue.*) I remember now how he was always looking through the fashion magazines. Sometimes he'd take them up to his room. He'd *study* them. I always wondered why.
MRS. HERGESHEIMER. But why would he stay up in his room making hats? And then keep them locked in his closet?
MRS. CROSBY. He . . . he's just peculiar. That's all. He's just

peculiar. I thought so, the first time I saw the man. He's too prim for a man. He's too tidy the way he keeps his room. It's just not natural.

MRS. HERGESHEIMER. Oh, I wish now we hadn't looked.

MRS. CROSBY. I had a perfect right.

MRS. HERGESHEIMER. I know, but . . .

MRS. CROSBY. Why, I think he's the most peculiar man I ever heard of. Why, I'd rather be harboring a Communist.

MRS. HERGESHEIMER. Oh, Mrs. Crosby, don't say that.

MRS. CROSBY. I would. I'd rather be harboring a Communist than a man who makes hats.

MRS. HERGESHEIMER. Why, there's nothing wrong with making hats. I don't see anything wrong with it. Why, lots of men make hats. Some of the finest designers there are are men. Why, of course.

MRS. CROSBY. But he kept them locked in his closet. He was ashamed of them. He was.

MRS. HERGESHEIMER. Maybe it's just a hobby with him. Some men knit, you know, because it helps their nerves.

MRS. CROSBY. I'm going to ask him to leave.

MRS. HERGESHEIMER. Oh, no, Mrs. Crosby. Don't do that.

MRS. CROSBY. I am. I'm going to ask him to leave. And I'm going to call the store he works at and tell them what kind of a freak they have working for them. Indeed I am.

MRS. HERGESHEIMER. Oh, I wouldn't do that. It's not against the law for a man to make hats. He hasn't done anything really wrong.

MRS. CROSBY. Why, a man who'd make hats and lock them up in his closet, there's no telling what kind of a person he is. He might do any kind of dangerous, crazy thing.

MRS. HERGESHEIMER. Oh, I don't think so, Mrs. Crosby. Really I don't.

MRS. CROSBY. I'd rather he was a Communist. At least you know what a Communist is up to. But a man that makes hats? What can you tell about such a creature?

MRS. HERGESHEIMER. I wouldn't give it another thought if I was you.

MRS. CROSBY. Well, I guess it takes all kinds of people to make a world.

MRS. HERGESHEIMER. Of course. That's the way to look at it.

MRS. CROSBY. Hats! Hats! Hats! With flowers on them.
MRS. HERGESHEIMER. I must run along now.
MRS. CROSBY. Hats!
MRS. HERGESHEIMER. Goodness, I hope he never finds out.
MRS. CROSBY. I don't care if he does. Just let him try to scold me, in that superior way of his. (*Imitating Mr. Newbold.*) "Mrs. Crosby, someone's been tampering with the lock on my closet. I demand privacy, Mrs. Crosby. That's all I ask is just one tiny closet to call my own. That's all I ask." Hmm. I'll have an answer for him. "What in God's name does a grown-up man like you mean by making hats, Mr. Newbold? Shame!" That's what I'll tell him. And he won't act so superior then. (*Mrs. Hergesheimer flutters out of the house as though wanting to avoid further involvement. Mrs. Crosby studies the hat once more, then takes it to the mirror and tries it on, looking at herself in it, assuming a variety of poses with the hat, at times mocking its elegance with a feeling of low burlesque. Then she tosses it on a chair and goes to the kitchen. After a few moments, Mr. Newbold comes out of the closet in which he has been hiding. He is a shattered man. All of his pride, his erect posture, his air of authority are gone. He has become a shy and frightened young girl. Lovingly, he picks up the hat and carries it to the mirror where he puts it on, looking at himself. He strikes one or two poses in an effort to create some image of beauty, but he does not succeed. The image has been destroyed for him. He drops the hat onto a chair, then himself falls onto the sofa and cries like a hopeless child.*)

CURTAIN

PROPERTY PLOT

On Stage

Assorted Victorian living room furniture
Telephone
Mirror, on wall

Off Stage

Woman's flowered hat (Mrs. Crosby)

Personal

Watch (Mr. Newbold)

MEMORY OF SUMMER

CHARACTERS

ALICE

VIOLA

COAST GUARD

MEMORY OF SUMMER

The time is late September, and the scene is the beach of a now-desolate resort. The sea presumably is at the left of the stage, and a wall, about shoulder-high, lines the back. Powerful waves crack against the shore. At the right are a few shops or stands that were full of noisy activity all summer, but now are boarded up, and an occasional wind goes whistling through their emptiness, sending the last bits of summer refuse (paper napkins, candy wrappers, etc.) scattering over the sand. It is a chilly day and the atmosphere is damp and gray. Viola comes through a gate in the wall at the back. She is a slim woman in her forties, with a delicate prettiness. There is a fragile smile on her face, a rather unrealistic smile that exists for itself. She wears an elegant cloak over her swimsuit and carries a large towel. Her feet are in sandals. She walks to the left of the stage, slowly, her eyes looking out at the sea. Then in the background can be heard the voice of the old housekeeper, Alice.)

ALICE. (*A worried voice, off.*) Miss Viola! Miss Viola!
VIOLA. (*Lightly.*) You needn't worry about me, Alice. (*Alice comes through the gate. She is a woman in her sixties. She is concerned and fretful.*)
ALICE. Oh, Miss Viola, *do* come back to the cottage! It's late September and there's a chill in the air. You shouldn't be going for a swim.
VIOLA. Why, it's a splendid day, Alice. And you know how I love the water. Sometimes the water is very warm on a day like this. Really it is. Why, this is a perfect day for a swim.
ALICE. Miss Viola, the summer's over . . .
VIOLA. Nonsense, Alice.
ALICE. The summer's long over, Miss Viola, and we should be returning home.
VIOLA. (*Blandly.*) Home?
ALICE. You have a husband and a fine home waiting for you in

Saint Louis, Miss Viola. Why don't you come back to the cottage with me now, and we'll make our reservations and start our packing.

VIOLA. (*A flicker of anguish on her face.*) It's my holiday, Alice.

ALICE. The holiday's over, Miss Viola. Can't I make you see? Can't you understand?

VIOLA. (*Gayly.*) My holiday isn't over. Why, I feel that it's just begun. I know the sky is a little dark now, but the water is still . . . quite warm. And you know how I love the sea. Every morning I must have my dip. It's the first thing I think of when I awaken: I'll have my breakfast, I tell myself, and then I'll hurry to the beach, where all the young people are laughing and playing and . . . (*She catches herself.*)

ALICE. (*Cautiously.*) Miss Viola . . . there aren't any young people here now. There's no one here now.

VIOLA. (*Forcing a little laugh.*) They're all sissies. They're afraid of the water, just because the sun is under. Don't they know they can't expect every day to be sunny and bright?

ALICE. Look, Miss Viola, the shops are all boarded up. The young lifeguards have all gone back to school. All the venders are gone, too. See? There's none of them around. You're all alone now. There's no one left but the Beach Patrol, and I'll have to call them if you go in the water, Miss Viola. I'll *have* to.

VIOLA. (*Laughing.*) Dear Alice! You sounded then just like you did when I was a child, and you had to call me in from play.

ALICE. I wish I could reason with you, Miss Viola.

VIOLA. You hurry back to the cottage, Alice. I want you to press my white piqué for me. I'm dining at the inn . . .

ALICE. (*Trying to protest.*) Miss Viola . . .

VIOLA. I'll be dining at the inn, and the inn will be full of young people, beautiful young people, dancing, and they mustn't point at me for looking dowdy and old. You don't want your Viola to be pointed at and scoffed at, do you, Alice? I want to look *young* for them, Alice. And I'll dance with the young men, too. And I'll laugh for them. And I'll tell my naughty little stories for them, my naughty-nice stories, to amuse them. For they mustn't think I am a prude. And I'll dance and laugh with them, while the little orchestra is playing those sweet, *sweet* melodies; and I'll come home long after midnight, simply exhausted, and fall into my lovely bed and let you cover me with soft, soft blankets . . .

ALICE. Miss Viola, there's no one at the inn. The orchestra played its last dance on Labor Day.
VIOLA. (*Gayly.*) . . . and put out my blue satin slippers and my nicest lingerie! And if the night air is a little chilly, I'll wear my furs . . . (*She goes running off into the water.*)
ALICE. (*Frantically calling.*) Miss Viola! Miss Viola! (*Suddenly there is the shrill sound of a whistle. Then a young Coast Guard scales the wall and lands gracefully on his feet. He is a young man of almost god-like handsomeness, still bronzed from the summer sun. He wears a beach helmet and the summer fatigue uniform of the Coast Guard.*)
COAST GUARD. (*To Alice.*) Is the lady *loco*?
ALICE. I wish someone could stop her.
COAST GUARD. She's been here every day. We saw her from the lookout. We're supposed to keep people off the beach after Labor Day, but we didn't want to say anything, as long as the weather was O.K. and the sea was smooth.
ALICE. I couldn't stop her.
COAST GUARD. (*Blows his whistle and calls after Viola.*) You gotta come in! You gotta come in! (*To Alice.*) She a good swimmer?
ALICE. Yes. She loves to swim. She's a very good swimmer.
COAST GUARD. The water's rough today and there's a stiff undercurrent. It's cold, too.
ALICE. I'm going back to the cottage and call her doctor. He told me to call him if she acted this way. He doesn't know what to do with the dear child.
COAST GUARD. (*Using hands as a megaphone.*) You gotta come in! You gotta come in!
ALICE. (*Handing him the beach blanket.*) Wrap her up in this. And here's a little brandy I brought along for her. (*Hands him a flask.*) She likes it and I thought it'd warm her. I'm going back to the cottage and call her doctor. (*She hurries off.*)
COAST GUARD. (*Walking to the water. Obviously Viola has started back. He calls to her.*) What *are* you, an Eskimo? (*He waits.*) The water's in the sixties. We can't let anyone go in the water this time of year. (*He still waits, holding up the blanket for her.*) Come on, let me wrap this around you. (*Viola comes out of the water, seeking her blanket.*)

VIOLA. I had a lovely swim. Really, the water was surprisingly warm. I had a lovely swim. (*She dries herself hurriedly.*)
COAST GUARD. We can't let you go in any more, lady. You gotta stop these little beach parties, at least until next season.
VIOLA. Next season?
COAST GUARD. (*Wrapping the blanket around her.*) Yah. This one's over.
VIOLA. Thank you, young man, for your attentions.
COAST GUARD. The next time you go in, I'll have to come in and get you.
VIOLA. You will?
COAST GUARD. Yes, ma'am. And I wouldn't like that at all.
VIOLA. But that's absurd. The sea is quite public. Certainly I have the right to go for my usual morning dip without making myself the cause of such concern.
COAST GUARD. Sorry, lady, but I can't let you go in any more.
VIOLA. I must say, I appreciate your thoughtfulness and concern. It's most gallant of you, but . . .
COAST GUARD. It's not gallant, lady. It's just my orders.
VIOLA. Oh!
COAST GUARD. I should have stopped you before this. If you were to drown, I'd get sent to the brig for not doing my duty.
VIOLA. I see. Well, I shouldn't wish to cause anyone trouble. (*She looks around nervously.*) Did Alice leave some brandy for me?
COAST GUARD. (*Handing her the flask.*) Here, ma'am.
VIOLA. Thank you. (*Takes a swallow.*) I wish I could offer *you* some.
COAST GUARD. I never drink on duty, ma'am.
VIOLA. Oh!
COAST GUARD. Thank you, just the same.
VIOLA. If you'd care to come by the cottage sometime, I'd gladly offer you a drink, when you were not on duty.
COAST GUARD. Thank you, ma'am. I very seldom go out here. When I'm off duty, I go into town.
VIOLA. Now, you probably are thinking I'm one of those horrid old women who go around flirting with handsome young men. Of course that's what you're thinking!
COAST GUARD. No, ma'am, I . . .
VIOLA. I insist on your understanding that where I come from, I

should have been considered most ungracious if I hadn't offered some little sign of hospitality to you . . . after your kindness.
COAST GUARD. Thank you, just the same.
VIOLA. Now where did Alice go?
COAST GUARD. Your maid returned to the cottage, ma'am.
VIOLA. Did she? And left you to stay and look after me?
COAST GUARD. Yes, ma'am, I . . .
VIOLA. Now, I should have brought my beach basket along. I had such gay times all summer long. Every day I brought a huge basket to the beach with me, full of the most delicious goodies, and always with a great Thermos full of daiquiris; and I always brought along a little radio, too, to provide cheerful music for the day. I held court, one might say, on the beach. I was hostess all day long to the young people.
COAST GUARD. I have to be getting back to the lookout, ma'am.
VIOLA. You . . . are a handsome young man, aren't you?
COAST GUARD. Am I? Thank you, ma'am.
VIOLA. Now you musn't think I'm being fresh again. You *don't*, do you?
COAST GUARD. No, ma'am, I . . .
VIOLA. I see no reason at all why I shouldn't say it. I *admire* a handsome young man, and men have never hesitated to tell me I was pretty, so I think it only fair in return for me to tell you that you're *very* handsome.
COAST GUARD. (*More embarrassed.*) Thank you.
VIOLA. From the water, I saw you scaling the wall after you had blown your rude whistle at me, and you were like a god.
COAST GUARD. A god?
VIOLA. Yes, like an angry sea god, scaling walls to save a disobedient naiad.
COAST GUARD. Oh.
VIOLA. A naiad is a water nymph. In Greek mythology.
COAST GUARD. Yes, ma'am.
VIOLA. A *nymph* to the Greeks was something entirely different from what the term implies today.
COAST GUARD. I . . . I don't know much about such things. (*Viola shivers.*) You better get back in your cottage, ma'am, and get warm.
VIOLA. Ah, but I *can't* leave my glorious beach.

COAST GUARD. You're cold, ma'am. You're shivering and your hands are trembling.
VIOLA. (*Looking at him blankly.*) Are they?
COAST GUARD. You need something to warm you.
VIOLA. I do?
ALICE. (*Off, calling.*) Miss Viola! Miss Viola!!
COAST GUARD. Here comes your maid, ma'am. I'll run along. (*He runs fleetly off.*)
VIOLA. (*Following a few steps after him, calling.*) Young man! Young man! (*Politely he returns.*)
COAST GUARD. Yes, ma'am?
VIOLA. (*Fumblingly.*) I . . . I feel I must thank you for looking after me.
COAST GUARD. That's all right, ma'am. Like I said, I was only carrying out orders.
VIOLA. It's very courteous of you to refuse my thanks, but, nevertheless, you have behaved with the most courageous thoughtfulness and . . . and valor and . . .
COAST GUARD. (*Quite puzzled by her.*) It was nothing, ma'am.
VIOLA. (*Taking his hand.*) Nevertheless . . . I wish to thank you from the bottom of my heart . . .
ALICE. (*Hurrying on.*) Miss Viola, you must come back to the cottage now. Your doctor's coming.
VIOLA. The young man says I need something to make me warm, Alice. (*She laughs.*)
ALICE. Of course you do. (*Nodding to the Coast Guard.*) I'll take her home now.
COAST GUARD. Good day! (*He runs off.*)
VIOLA. (*Hovering in Alice's arms.*) The young man said I needed something to make me warm.
ALICE. There's a log fire going in the cabin. I'll have a hot tub ready for you and then a cup of broth. Your doctor insists that you go into the city. He's going to take you to see another doctor, Miss Viola. Now be reasonable.
VIOLA. (*In a faraway voice, looking about her.*) Where are all the young people today, Alice?
ALICE. They're gone.
VIOLA. Gone?
ALICE. Yes, dear! They've all gone back to school.
VIOLA. But, this is where the young people belong, on a sunny

beach, surrounded by clear blue water and splashing waves . . . laughing and playing in the sand.
ALICE. The season's over, Miss Viola.
VIOLA. And you must get out my white piqué for me to wear to the inn tonight, Alice.
ALICE. But your doctor's coming, Miss Viola. Here, dear, keep the blanket around you. You're shivering.
VIOLA. The young man said I needed something to keep me warm.
ALICE. (*Leading her off.*) Yes, dear. We'll go back to the cottage and hug the cozy fire until your doctor comes.
VIOLA. And tonight I must look my best for the young people. I shall delight them with my stories, and I shall dance more gayly than any of them. And I shall wear my blue satin slippers, and my lovely furs, if the night air is at all chilly . . .
ALICE. Yes, Miss Viola.
VIOLA. (*As they go off, Alice hugs her close to her.*) And tomorrow will be a lovely day at the beach. The bright sun will beat down on us and warm us through and through, but we can always run into the breakers and have a quick, cool dip to refresh us, can't we? And all the beautiful young people will be laughing and playing together in the sand . . .

CURTAIN

PROPERTY PLOT

On Stage

Beach refuse (napkins, candy wrappers, etc.)

Personal

Large beach towel-blanket (Viola)
Flask (Alice)

BUS RILEY'S BACK IN TOWN

CHARACTERS

SALESMAN

HOWIE

JACKIE LOOMIS

BERNICE HENRY

RALPH HENRY

BUS RILEY

BUS RILEY'S BACK IN TOWN

The scene of the play is the Fiesta Room of the Hotel Boomerang in a small town in middle Texas. The Fiesta Room is only the bar of the hotel, and as a bar not a very satisfactory one, being permitted to sell only beer. But the décor pretends, at least, to an air of festivity, with symbols of primitive Mexican culture. Mexican hats and serapes hang on the wall, there is a big poster of a bullfight, and the doors to the toilets are marked, one Señora, the other Señor. But there is not much festivity in the Fiesta Room at present. Only one customer is in view, a salesman, sitting at the bar, drinking a glass of beer and reading an evening paper. Howie, the bartender, an easygoing man of middle age, stays behind the bar, not even pretending to keep busy.

SALESMAN. Used t'be I'd come into this town and sell maybe five thousand dollars' worth of merchandise in one day.
HOWIE. Bet ya don't do that now, do you?
SALESMAN. No. I'm doin' good now if I make my expenses in this town. I ain't kiddin'.
HOWIE. Yah. Things ain't what they used to be around here. That drought didn't help it any.
SALESMAN. Yah. That drought was bad.
HOWIE. But this little town really had it once.
SALESMAN. It sure did. (*He looks around the room.*) This all the customers ya got, Howie?
HOWIE. It's early in the week. We don't do enough business to stay open, except on Friday and Saturday nights. There's always a crowd in here then.
SALESMAN. Things have sure changed. They sure have.
HOWIE. The business we do on weekends has to carry us through the week. It's the hotel's worry. Not mine. They wanta keep the room open just for the looks of things. When we have a losing week, I guess they make up for it with the dining room. The dining room does a pretty good business.

SALESMAN. Yah. It's about the only place in town you can get decent food. All you can get in these lunch stands around here is greaser food—chili and tamales. I can't eat it. (*Now a young girl comes running into the room from the outside. She is Jackie Loomis, a quite pretty girl of twenty-three or twenty-four, wearing a simple summer wash frock, spectator pumps and no stockings. There is something taut about her, a breathlessness that makes her seem to live every moment as though it were a crisis. She runs to the bar excitedly and speaks to Howie.*)
JACKIE. (*In a somewhat private voice.*) Howie, is it true Bus Riley's in town?
HOWIE. Yes, Jackie. At least, he was in town a day or so ago. His father, you know, has been real sick, and Bus had to come home to give him blood transfusions. Bus has been spending most of his time at the hospital, they say.
JACKIE. Has he been in here, Howie?
HOWIE. Yes, a few times. Usually comes in at night and has a few beers.
JACKIE. What's he like now, Howie?
HOWIE. Like? Well, I . . . uh . . .
JACKIE. Is he still a *god?*
HOWIE. (*Chuckles.*) Well, I don't know I'd say he was a *god.* He looked pretty much like the same old Bus to me. The only difference I could see was he was wearing a sailor suit.
JACKIE. I've just *got* to see him, Howie. I've just *got* to.
HOWIE. (*At a loss for what to say.*) Well, Jackie, I . . .
JACKIE. Don't tell anyone, Howie. Please don't tell anyone I asked about him. Will you promise?
HOWIE. No. I won't tell, Jackie.
JACKIE. Is he staying at home, do you know, Howie?
HOWIE. As far as I know, Jackie.
JACKIE. (*Digs into her purse for a piece of change.*) Give me a dime, Howie.
HOWIE. You bet, Jackie. (*She takes the dime from him and hurries into the telephone booth in a corner.*)
SALESMAN. (*An observant man.*) That was Del Loomis's daughter, wasn't it?
HOWIE. Yep!
SALESMAN. How is old Del these days?
HOWIE. The same, I guess. No one ever sees him.

SALESMAN. Dead drunk, I suppose.
HOWIE. I suppose. They keep a nurse with him mosta the time.
SALESMAN. Just think. He built this hotel, din he?
HOWIE. Built mosta the buildings in town.
SALESMAN. And now, they tell me, he don't have a nickel.
HOWIE. Dead drunk. Dead broke. Poor old Del.
SALESMAN. Yah. Well, he had it once, though.
HOWIE. Yah. Del had millions.
SALESMAN. Lived like a lord.
HOWIE. Had a whole fleet of automobiles, two ranches, swimming pool, fifty servants, several airplanes. Kept a yacht down in the Gulf.
SALESMAN. Yah. It just don't seem possible that a man can have as much as old Del did and then lose it.
HOWIE. Del Loomis just about made this town. He ran things here pretty much the way he wanted 'em. We all kowtowed to him.
SALESMAN. It was a one-man town.
HOWIE. Yah! When Del had it, all of us here were prosperous, working in his oil field and at the ranches. He kept things humming. Then he lost it, and so did the rest of us. I guess we all owe a lot to Del, and he was a likable man, too, in a way. I mean he was always friendly when he met you on the street. But I guess all that money and all that power kinda went to his head. He was actin' kinda crazy around here, like he was Nero or one of those Roman emperors.
SALESMAN. Yah. I think Del was goin' off his rocker. That's what I think. (*He nods in the direction of Jackie, who is still in the telephone booth.*) That the daughter there was all the talk about? (*Howie nods a little reluctantly.*) In love with some fellow Del didn't want her to marry, wasn't she?
HOWIE. That's it. The story got in all the papers. It all happened five or six years ago.
SALESMAN. This is the first time I ever saw her. She sure is a looker.
HOWIE. Del was crazy about her. He acted to me like he was jealous of the boy and in love with her himself. (*Two young people come in: Ralph and Bernice Henry, a married couple, friends of Jackie. A little mystified, they are looking for her.*)
BERNICE. (*To Howie.*) Did Jackie come in here?

HOWIE. (*Nodding to the telephone booth.*) In there, Bernice.
BERNICE. Oh. (*Jackie, seeing Bernice and Ralph, hurries out of the booth, a little embarrassed with a feeling of having been caught.*)
JACKIE. Oh, I was just calling home, Bee. I . . . I just remembered that Daddy asked me to. He said maybe he'd want me to bring something home from town.
BERNICE. (*A little miffed.*) Well, you might have told us. Ralph and I were looking all over for you after the movie let out. You made off in such a hurry. I thought we'd come over here together. We always do.
JACKIE. I . . . I'm sorry, Bee.
RALPH. What's the difference? Let's sit down and have a beer. (*He leads Bernice to a booth on the side of the room opposite the bar, calling to Howie on the way.*) Three beers, Howie!
BERNICE. (*Still a little peeved at Jackie.*) Maybe you want to get rid of Ralph and me.
JACKIE. No, Bee. Honest! It's just that I remembered suddenly that I'd promised Daddy to call. Honest!
BERNICE. (*Looking at her a little dubiously.*) Well, I don't see why you had to go running off that way, without even saying a word. (*She sits next to Ralph in the booth. Then Jackie joins them, sitting opposite them.*)
RALPH. (*To Bernice.*) It doesn't make any difference, Mama. We're not Jackie's guardians, or anything. (*Howie goes over and sets down three beers for them.*)
BERNICE. Oh, did you order beer for me? I'm not sure I want it. It makes me feel so logy in hot weather.
HOWIE. Want me to take it back?
BERNICE. No. I'll drink it. Darn! I wish you could order a Tom Collins in this town, or a gin and tonic. (*Howie returns to the bar.*) Lord, that was a putrid movie. Now, when they try to make an ancient Egyptian princess out of Lana Turner, I just don't believe it. I don't care what you say, I don't believe it. She's about as Egyptian as our Scotty. Did you like the picture, Jackie?
JACKIE. I . . . I didn't pay much attention to it.
BERNICE. Jackie, you're so nervous these days, I don't know what to make of you.
JACKIE. I'm not usually, Bee. It's just tonight. I . . . I guess I *am* a little nervous tonight.

BERNICE. What about?
JACKIE. I . . . I don't know, Bee. Just nervous. That's all.
BERNICE. Now, Jackie honey, you wanta look after yourself, and when you find yourself getting nervous, go home and relax. Take it easy. Isn't that what you say, Ralph?
RALPH. Sure. Take it easy. That's my motto.
JACKIE. (*A little annoyed by Bernice's assumed authority.*) It's nothing to get worried about, Bee.
BERNICE. Did you like the movie, Ralph?
RALPH. I liked the photography. The color was pretty.
BERNICE. That's all you care about. The photography. I like a story that's *real,* that shows just how nasty people really are, and doesn't mince words about it.
RALPH. Can't a movie be real if it shows people being nice, too?
BERNICE. Maybe. But what's the point? I mean . . .
JACKIE. (*Suddenly jumping up from her seat.*) Pardon me a minute, kids, will you?
BERNICE. Oh . . . sure. (*Jackie disappears into the door marked* Señora. *Bernice watches her and now reports to Ralph.*) Do you know what she's going to do?
RALPH. Well, I take it for granted that when a girl pardons herself to go to the ladies' room, that she's going to do one of two things.
BERNICE. (*Shaking her head wisely.*) Huh-uh. She's got you fooled. I know what she's going to do. She's going to take another of those pills.
RALPH. What pills?
BERNICE. Those sleeping pills she carries around with her.
RALPH. Honey, you keep telling me she takes sleeping pills, but if she does, why doesn't she ever go to sleep?
BERNICE. Ralph, don't you know anything about these things? She gets *high* on them, just like on liquor. Honest. I bet anything she's taking a pill now and just doesn't want us to know. You know why she ditched us after the movie, don't you?
RALPH. I'm perfectly willing to believe that she had to come over here to call her father.
BERNICE. Oh, you just don't know that girl. She came over here in hopes of finding Bus Riley. And she didn't want us to be around when she found him, either. And that wasn't her father

she was calling when we came in. Huh-uh. She was calling Bus's house. I bet anything.
RALPH. Well, what if she was? What's it to you?
BERNICE. It just so happens that Jackie Loomis is my oldest, dearest friend. And I know all that she's been through. I just want to spare her from going through anything more . . . with that . . . that half-breed Bus Riley.
RALPH. You think she still loves him?
BERNICE. Of course she does. She's been jumpy as a cat, ever since she heard he was back. She's just been dying to find some excuse to see him.
RALPH. After . . . everything that happened?
BERNICE. Of course. (*Jackie comes out of the ladies' room now. She seems quite merry. She lingers by the juke box, studying the selections, then going to the open door to see if Bus can be seen anywhere down the street.*)
RALPH. My God, the guy's been in prison since then . . .
BERNICE. I know, but she's still crazy about him. Besides, it was her father sent Bus to prison. She knows that. (*She makes sure that Jackie cannot overhear her.*) Bus wasn't really guilty of anything. I mean, Jackie was as much to blame for getting pregnant as Bus was. Even if he was a year older. It was just old-man Loomis's way of getting revenge. He certainly wasn't going to let her marry Bus. Bus, half-Mexican, from the other side of the tracks.
RALPH. Bus was a pretty nice guy, though, honey. At least, when I knew him.
BERNICE. I'm not saying he wasn't. Still, he had a Mexican mother . . .
RALPH. But she's a very nice woman. I mean . . .
BERNICE. He lived out at the edge of town in that ugly little shanty full of kids.
RALPH. That's just because his old man wouldn't go to work.
BERNICE. All right. But what difference did that make to Del Loomis, when he was the richest man in middle Texas? He wouldn't have stood for Jackie marrying anyone like that. Why, Del Loomis was even trying to get Jackie married off to some European nobility.
RALPH. Del Loomis is a crackpot.
BERNICE. Maybe he is. But that doesn't keep the situation from

being hopeless. It's just no good for Jackie to be getting excited all over again about Bus Riley. I don't know why he had to come back to town.
RALPH. His old man was about to die.
BERNICE. Yes, and you know why, don't you? Got stabbed in one of those Mexican joints he hangs out in, and lost almost all his blood.
RALPH. Well . . . you can't keep her from seeing Bus if she really wants to.
BERNICE. I can try. (*Jackie rejoins them at the booth, Bernice becomes suddenly very silent.*)
JACKIE. Oh, I don't want to go home tonight. I feel like I'd like to stay here until it closes. I don't want to go home.
BERNICE. Jackie, you can't stay here all alone. People would talk.
JACKIE. What difference would that make? People talk about me already.
BERNICE. That's not so, Jackie. You just imagine it.
JACKIE. (*With a quick little look at Bernice.*) Do I?
BERNICE. Yes. Of course you do.
JACKIE. Well . . . maybe I do.
RALPH. I'm about ready for bed now, aren't you, Mother?
BERNICE. Yes, and we've got to relieve the baby-sitter.
JACKIE. Oh, let's not go yet. Please, let's not go yet.
BERNICE. Jackie, there's no point in sitting in this dump all evening. Come on over to our house if you want to. You can have a beer there. Or Ralph could fix you something stronger.
JACKIE. No thanks, Bee. You'll be busy looking after the children. I . . . I won't bother you. (*Now Bus Riley enters. Jackie is aware of him the moment he comes through the door, and Bernice sees a look come into her eyes. Bus is a very handsome young man of twenty-four or twenty-five, with sleek black hair and just a suggestion of Latin features and coloring. He wears his Navy whites with splendor. He calls to Howie as soon as he enters, not noticing the people in the booth.*)
BUS. Draw me a beer, Howie! (*He strides to the bar.*) Well, the Old Man's on the way to recovery now. I'm clearin' outa here in the morning.
HOWIE. Leavin' us so soon, Bus?

BUS. Yah. I've had enough of this town, forever. (*He drinks his beer. Bernice and Ralph get up from the booth.*)
BERNICE. Let's go, Jackie. (*Jackie sits almost as though wounded by the sight and sound of Bus.*)
JACKIE. Well, I . . .
BERNICE. You can't stay here, Jackie. You know you can't.
RALPH. Come along, Jackie old girl.
JACKIE. (*Reluctantly rising to her feet.*) Well . . . if you say so . . . I . . .
RALPH. (*To Bernice.*) I'll pay the bill. You and Jackie go on out to the car.
BERNICE. O.K., honey. (*Like a protecting angel, Bernice hovers about Jackie, getting her out of the bar before Bus sees her. At the bar, Ralph lays down a bill for Howie and gives Bus a hearty slap on the back.*)
RALPH. Hello, Riley! Good to see you back.
BUS. Oh . . . Ralph Henry! Hi ya, Ralph? (*They shake hands.*)
RALPH. How's your father?
BUS. Gettin' along O.K. now. Doc says he's outa danger.
RALPH. Good. Glad to hear it. Well . . . nice to've seen you, Bus.
BUS. Yah . . . thanks, Ralph. (*Ralph goes out now. Bus is still trying to identify him.*) Let's see. He married Bernice Cain, didn't he?
HOWIE. Right. She just went out . . . with an old friend of yours.
BUS. Who? You mean . . . ?
HOWIE. Yah. She was sitting right over there when you came in.
BUS. I'll be damned. Well . . . maybe it's a good thing I din see her. Know anywhere I could get a bottle of whiskey, Howie? I been cooped up in that hospital room for so long, I feel like celebratin' a little before I leave town.
HOWIE. You can't buy hard liquor in this county, Bus. You'll have to drive over to the next county, buy it there.
BUS. It was Del Loomis had that law passed, wasn't it?
HOWIE. I guess so.
BUS. He stayed home getting plastered, but thought the county should stay dry. That hypocrite son of a bitch! (*He shows intense hatred and anger.*) Well, I'm goin' from here to Galveston. Things are a li'l different down there.

HOWIE. I hear things are wide open in Galveston.
SALESMAN. I hear they got gambling down there, and women.
BUS. You can get anything you want there. *Any*thing.
HOWIE. That where the Navy's been keepin' you all this time, Bus? Galveston?
BUS. Christ no! I've been everywhere there is to go. Around the world twice. I'm joining a new ship in Galveston. We sail for Hong Kong next week.
SALESMAN. (*His love of adventure stirred.*) Hong Kong!
BUS. Howie, what's the situation with girls in this town? The same as with whiskey?
HOWIE. (*Laughs and begins to ponder the question.*) Well, let me think, Bus.
BUS. How about Melba Freeman? She still around?
HOWIE. No. Melba got herself a job in Dallas. Left here a few years ago.
BUS. Oh. That's too bad. Well . . . how 'bout Maxine Tucker? Where's she?
HOWIE. Oh, she's married, Bus. Married Lyn Overton. Remember him? They got two kids now. Happy as can be.
BUS. Oh . . . that's great. Uh . . . whatever happened to Rosamund Skinner? There was a beauty.
HOWIE. Rose got killed in a auto accident, Bus. About a year ago. She and the boy she was with.
BUS. Oh, gee, that's too bad.
HOWIE. I'm afraid I can't think of anyone now, Bus. The town's pretty quiet now.
BUS. What the hell! I'll go down to the Mexican quarter. I can pick up a chick there.
HOWIE. I can give you a shot to go with that beer, if you want it, Bus.
BUS. *Do* I?
HOWIE. I always keep a bottle back here to celebrate with. And this is an occasion, you being home. (*He pours out a jigger which Bus grabs instantly and downs.*)
BUS. Thanks, Howie.
HOWIE. How're things, Bus? I mean, on the level.
BUS. O.K. *now*, Howie. I mean . . . well, they kept me in the cage for a year's all. I . . . I just don't think about it any more. The minute I got out, I made up my mind, I was never gonna

think about it again. So . . . I'm in the Navy now and life is great. Sure. I get my kicks. Uh . . . Howie, how 'bout another shot of that stuff? That's the first real drink I've had since I got here; and man, I need it!

HOWIE. Sure, Bus. (*He pours another, which Bus immediately downs.*)

BUS. Thanks, Howie. You're a pal. If you could only find me a girl, you'd be a *real* pal.

HOWIE. I might do that. (*Bus looks at him questioningly.*) Jackie's been asking me about you, Bus.

BUS. Has she?

HOWIE. She was calling you from here before Ralph and Bernice came in.

BUS. I guess I'd left the house.

HOWIE. I think she'd like to see you, Bus.

BUS. What's she like now, Howie?

HOWIE. Still the same sweet kid, Bus, and prettier'n ever.

BUS. Yah?

HOWIE. I bet she comes back here after she gets rid of Ralph and Bernice. I bet anything.

BUS. I'm not sure I'd know how to act around her now.

HOWIE. (*Looking out the front window.*) I was right. There she is now, pulling up at the curb. She let Ralph and Bernice take her home, then got into her own car and came right back. I told you she wanted to see you.

BUS. (*This is a troubled moment for Bus, not knowing whether he can face her or not.*) Howie, I don't know if I can . . .

HOWIE. What d'ya mean, Bus?

BUS. (*Making a start to get away.*) I'm heading out the back way. I can't see Jackie again.

HOWIE. (*Catching Bus at the end of the bar.*) Hold on, Bus. Hold on. She'll feel awful bad if you run off. (*Bus says nothing. He just stays where he is, his back to the door, his head down, dreading to face her. Jackie comes in. She is a little hesitant, a little uncertain of her welcome. She goes half the distance toward Bus before speaking. The salesman watches with curiosity.*)

JACKIE. Bus? (*Bus turns to face her now. He has caught hold of himself and has a big smile for her.*)

BUS. Jackie!

JACKIE. How are you, Bus?

BUS. Couldn't be better, Doll. Step right up here and have a beer. Long time no see. How ya doin'?
JACKIE. (*Joining him at the bar.*) I'm all right, Bus. (*Howie sets another beer before her.*)
BUS. By God, you're still the best lookin' doll I ever saw.
JACKIE. Thank you, Bus. You look wonderful. Really!
BUS. It's the monkey suit. The girls always go for it.
JACKIE. (*More serious now.*) Bus . . . I just had to see you. Why didn't you call me, Bus?
BUS. Well . . . I din know whether a call from me'd be very appreciated, Jackie.
JACKIE. Oh, Bus, it would have been. Honest, Bus, nothing that happened . . . was my fault. You know how Daddy is. It . . . it just made me sick, what happened.
BUS. Drink your beer, Doll.
JACKIE. I was praying you'd call me, Bus. I wanted so to hear your voice . . . to see you again . . . .
BUS. I ran into trouble with your old man once, Jackie. I din want to again.
JACKIE. There's no reason to be afraid of him any more. He's changed.
BUS. Yah?
JACKIE. You know . . . he drinks. He . . . he doesn't know much that goes on any more. I . . . I do anything I want to now.
BUS. Well, that's great. You got your car outside? How 'bout drivin' over to the next county and pickin' up a bottle? We could stop at the Riverview, maybe, if it's still runnin'.
JACKIE. It is. My car's outside. Dance with me, Bus.
BUS. Dance? Here?
JACKIE. (*Running to the juke box to drop a nickel to play her favorite tune.*) Yes. Please.
BUS. O.K. We'll dance. (*The music starts, and he takes her in his arms. They dance slowly and softly to the love song, neither of them speaking for a while.*)
SALESMAN. (*Softly to Howie.*) That the boy . . . all the trouble was about?
HOWIE. Yah. That's him.
SALESMAN. And Del had him sent to prison?
HOWIE. Oh, it was a great big fluke. The boy was eighteen

when it happened. The girl was seventeen. So, according to law, the girl was a minor and the boy wasn't. They sent him to some reform school, but they let him go after about a year. He's no criminal, and they knew it. If you ask me, Del's the one they shoulda sent to prison.

SALESMAN. Yah. Gimme another beer, Howie. (*Howie gives him a glass of beer and then begins to wash and dry glasses. The salesman is content to sit drinking his beer, just watching the two young people dance. Both Jackie and Bus have been silent in each other's arms. Now Jackie, as though rising out of a heavenly dream, speaks.*)

JACKIE. Oh, Bus, I've been telling myself all day that maybe I'd see you tonight, and maybe be dancing with you again, after all these years.

BUS. Yah. It's great, Doll.

JACKIE. Bus . . . I missed you terribly after you'd gone.

BUS. Yah? Well . . . same here.

JACKIE. I was so afraid you'd think it was my fault . . . what happened.

BUS. No, Doll. I never blamed it on you.

JACKIE. Oh, Bus, I missed you so, I was afraid I'd go crazy. Honest. I wanted to talk to you, just to talk to you, and be with you. Why didn't you answer my letters, Bus?

BUS. Hell, Jackie. I didn't know what to say.

JACKIE. I know.

BUS. (*Trying to sound more cheerful.*) Hey, I thought you'd be an old married woman by now.

JACKIE. No.

BUS. How come?

JACKIE. Oh, I've dated a few boys since you left, but they didn't seem to mean anything.

BUS. (*In a tone of inquiry.*) Yah?

JACKIE. (*Daring to ask it.*) How 'bout you, Bus? Have . . . have you fallen in love with anyone?

BUS. No. Not me. I don't fall in love any more. (*They have stopped dancing now and stand far away from the bar, clinging to each other, talking in soft, repressed voices.*)

JACKIE. Bus, I'll always remember when we first started going together.

BUS. (*A memory he has not tried to recall.*) Oh . . . yah.
JACKIE. Remember how shy we were of each other for so long?
BUS. Yah. I remember.
JACKIE. You used to walk me home from school in the afternoon, and we'd sit together on my doorstep for *hours,* and not say a word.
BUS. (*Obviously not giving himself to the recall.*) Sure, sure.
JACKIE. And the first time you kissed me. Oh, I'll never forget. Remember how scared we were when we made love, feeling so guilty and afraid. You used to tell me I was like some wonderful princess . . .
BUS. I'd forgotten I was so corny.
JACKIE. But we really felt those things, Bus. And when you really feel them, they're *not* corny. And I used to think of you as a god. I did. When we studied about Greece in Ancient History, and read about their gods and goddesses, I always visualized you, Bus, as Mercury, and Mars, and Apollo.
BUS. Well . . . I guess you had me wrong, Doll.
JACKIE. Oh, Bus, I was in love with you. I've been in love with you ever since, all these years. Every time I went out with another boy, I was mad because he wasn't you.
BUS. (*Turning it into a joke.*) Hey, I guess I feel flattered.
JACKIE. All these years I've been wanting to tell you. I'm still in love with you, Bus. I guess I always will be.
BUS. Well . . . that's great. You know I think a lotta *you,* too, Doll. I sure as hell do.
JACKIE. Did you ever know what happened to me, Bus? Daddy took me to some doctor in Forth Worth, and I had an abortion. Oh, Bus, it was terrible. I almost died. I really wanted to die, Bus. I wanted the baby so bad. (*Bus is not capable of dealing with this outpouring of sorrows. He is at a loss for words.*)
BUS. Jackie, I . . . I just don't know what to say.
JACKIE. And then I came back here and heard what had happened to you. Oh Bus, I was despondent. I . . . I tried to kill myself, Bus. I did. Then Daddy sent me to a mental hospital in Kansas. I was there for about a year. For a long time, they wouldn't even let me out of my room without a guard.
BUS. (*Feeling more at a loss.*) Yah . . . well, look, Doll, it's not doing any good, goin' over all this . . .

JACKIE. I've wanted to tell you, Bus. I've wanted to tell you for so long now.
BUS. O.K., now you've told me. I been through bad times, too. Let's forget it. What d'ya say?
JACKIE. Kiss me, Bus. (*There is a hesitant pause.*) It's all right. I don't care if they see us. Kiss me.
BUS. Sure, Doll! (*Eagerly, he takes her in his arms and kisses her long and satisfyingly.*) How was that, Doll?
JACKIE. (*Clinging to him.*) Oh, Bus!
BUS. You still know how to cuddle, don't you, Doll?
JACKIE. Bus, don't make fun.
BUS. Who says I'm makin' fun? Look, Doll, you wait here a minute while I make a telephone call, will ya? (*She stays planted as Bus hurries to the telephone booth. Howie and the salesman have other things to talk about now.*)
SALESMAN. Ya know, it always depresses me, kinda, to come back to this town now. It's so run-down now, compared with what it used to be. It used to be such a pretty town, with all them fine homes on Maple Street, a fine car settin' in every driveway, the lawns all trim and green.
HOWIE. Yah. Things change.
SALESMAN. They sure as hell do. Mosta them homes now are boarding houses, aren't they?
HOWIE. The Baker home is a funeral parlor.
SALESMAN. Yah. One of the finest houses in town and now it's a funeral parlor. This hotel's run-down, too. They don't even have a porter. It used to be a fine place to stay, but now it's the crummiest hotel on my route.
HOWIE. Wouldn't doubt it.
SALESMAN. Gimme one more beer, Howie. Then I'm goin' to bed. (*Howie draws another beer and sets it before him. Bus now comes hurrying from the telephone booth to report to Jackie.*)
BUS. Look, Doll, they got a cabin for us at the Riverview. Why don't we pile in your car, drive into the next county and pick up a bottle, and then stop at the Riverview and throw a ball. What d'ya say, Doll?
JACKIE. (*Dumbly.*) The Riverview?
BUS. Sure, Doll! Look, I've been cooped up with the Old Man all week now, and I wanta let off a little steam. Let's get goin', Doll.

JACKIE. (*Shattered with disillusionment, she sobs and runs to the door.*) No. I don't want to go to the Riverview with you, or anywhere else.
BUS. Well, for cryin' out loud! (*He goes to her patiently.*) Look, Doll, what's got into you all of a sudden?
JACKIE. Bus, you used to love me. I know you did. But you can't even pretend to now. You've just been making up polite answers to everything I've said. I'm just any other girl to you now that you can . . . can let off steam with, and then forget.
BUS. O.K., Doll. I'm not gonna talk you into it.
JACKIE. Oh, Bus, can't you remember the way we used to feel?
BUS. Maybe I don't want to.
JACKIE. (*Hurt.*) Oh, Bus!
BUS. Come off it, Jackie. Come off it.
JACKIE. Goodbye, Bus. (*She hurries outside now, and Bus makes a slow return to the bar. Howie is watching him, getting out his private bottle to pour him another shot.*)
HOWIE. Thought you might need this.
BUS. You're a pal. What the hell am I gonna do with myself till morning?
HOWIE. How about goin' home and goin' to bed?
BUS. I couldn't get to sleep. I come back to this little town, and I remember too many things to sleep. I just keep wantin' to get away, to get away.
HOWIE. There's the Mexican Quarter. Some of those places stay open all night.
BUS. Yah. (*Picks up the shot of whiskey.*) Gimme a beer to chase this down with, Howie.
HOWIE. O.K.
BUS. B'lieve me, when I clear outa this town tomorrow, it's for good. (*He downs the whiskey and begins drinking his beer. By this time the salesman is asleep, his head lying in one arm, curved over the bar. He snores and Howie taps him on the shoulder. The salesman stirs.*)
SALESMAN. Huh? What . . . ? Oh, have I been asleep? What d'ya know? Well, I hope I'll be able to do that when I get into bed. What do I owe you, Howie?
HOWIE. One-ten.
SALESMAN. (*Taking money from his pocket.*) There ya are.

(*Gets up from stool.*) Ho hum! Gotta get up in the morning and see my customers. Wish business was better. I sure do.
HOWIE. Good night, Harry. (*The salesman goes off, wandering through the archway leading into the hotel lobby.*)
BUS. I'll finish this up in a minute, Howie, and let you close. (*He takes a long drink of beer.*)
HOWIE. No hurry, Bus. Take your time. I gotta stay open till midnight, anyway, whether there's customers or not. (*Bus wanders over to the juke box and drops a nickel, then wanders back to the bar. A slow, mean blues begins to play, full of a rasping trumpet.*)
BUS. Did ya ever feel . . . like ya had to destroy something . . . in order to live?
HOWIE. No . . . no. I can't say that I ever felt that way, exactly.
BUS. I do. Maybe it's just a part of growin' up. (*Now Jackie wanders back into the Fiesta Room. There is a shyness, a hesitancy about her. Howie is the first to see her.*)
HOWIE. You leave something behind, Jackie? (*Now Bus turns around immediately to see her.*)
BUS. Jackie!
JACKIE. Bus . . . (*He hurries to her side, in the doorway.*)
BUS. You makin' a return engagement?
JACKIE. Bus . . . I'll go with you.
BUS. You will?
JACKIE. Sure. I'll go.
BUS. Look, Jackie, maybe we better not.
JACKIE. I want to, Bus. I do.
BUS. How about all this love talk?
JACKIE. I won't say those things any more. I promise.
BUS. They just don't go any more, Jackie. They just don't go.
JACKIE. (*With a little laugh of deprecation.*) I know . . .
BUS. Love, to me, is something they put you in jail for.
JACKIE. A doctor at the hospital told me . . . I was too sentimental about things.
BUS. I'm in this business now strictly for kicks, Doll.
JACKIE. I'll be . . . just an ordinary girl . . . you happen to pick up . . . and we'll throw a ball.
BUS. That's it, Doll. (*He grabs her to him hungrily and presses a sensual kiss against her lips. The music from the juke box makes*

a mocking accompaniment. Then he throws a bill on the counter for Howie.) So long, Dad! *(Bus wraps Jackie in his arms and they hurry out together. Howie watches them, drying glasses.)*

CURTAIN

PROPERTY PLOT

On Stage

Bar and stools
Whiskey bottles and shot glass, under bar
Beer bottles and glasses
Mexican hats, serapes and bullfight poster, on wall
Juke box
Telephone booth
"Señor" and "Señora" signs, on toilet doors

Personal

Newspaper (Salesman)
Purse, with money (Jackie)
Money (Ralph, Salesman, Bus)

THE RAINY AFTERNOON

CHARACTERS

WILMA

BILLIE MAE

VIC

THE RAINY AFTERNOON

The scene is the interior of an old barn in a small Midwestern town. Outside it is raining a slow, constant drizzle. Inside the barn, two little girls, dressed in stolen fragments of their mothers' clothing, play at having tea, making the barn an imaginary house, using nail kegs and tool chests and barrels for furniture. At left is a crude stairway leading up to a loft that is totally darkened. Of the two girls, Wilma is the older and more aggressive. She is perhaps ten. Billie Mae is only seven or eight. She plays the game with some uncertainty, as though she were depending on Wilma for instruction. Both girls have their dolls beside them, treating the dolls like children.

WILMA. You've got to spank your baby to make her behave.
BILLIE MAE. Mine's behaving.
WILMA. No she isn't. She's crying all the time. Spank her. I spank mine all the time. See? (*Wilma demonstrates.*)
BILLIE MAE. Mine isn't crying.
WILMA. She is, *too.* Spank her!
BILLIE MAE. Well, all right! (*Timidly she spanks her doll.*)
WILMA. . . . and scold her.
BILLIE MAE. You're a bad baby. You're a bad baby.
WILMA. (*Resuming her role.*) I guess you weren't invited to the big party at the country club yesterday. All the society people were there. I wore a beautiful new dress to it. Mrs. Sylvester Jones was there. She's a cow. She was dressed in horrible clothes. And her manners are terrible.
BILLIE MAE. Are they?
WILMA. Yes. Mrs. Sylvester Jones is a terrible woman. I don't know why anyone invites her any place. I didn't even speak to her.
BILLIE MAE. I wanta go home.
WILMA. (*Her own voice.*) You can't.
BILLIE MAE. Why not?
WILMA. Because we're having a tea party, silly. You can't just get up and walk out of a tea party.

BILLIE MAE. I'm not having any fun.
WILMA. You don't know how to *play.* (*Vic Bates, a boy of Wilma's age, pulls up at the door on his bicycle.*)
VIC. What're you crazy girls doin'?
WILMA. What business is it of yours?
VIC. I just asked. I don't care what you're doin'.
WILMA. Then go away. Our mothers don't allow us to play with boys.
BILLIE MAE. (*Affirming.*) No. You go away.
VIC. Am I hurtin' anyone, just sittin' here on my bike?
WILMA. I thought you crazy boys were goin' on a hike.
VIC. Don't you see it's raining?
WILMA. (*Making a face.*) Yah, yah, yah!
VIC. What've you got on your mothers' clothes for?
WILMA. We can put on our mothers' clothes if we want to, can't we, crazy?
VIC. I don't know what fun you crazy girls get outa playin' with dolls.
WILMA. Girls have as much fun as boys do.
BILLIE MAE. Yes. Girls have just as much fun as boys do.
VIC. (*Getting off his bike, coming into the barn.*) My father just got a new De Soto.
WILMA. *My* father got a Pontiac.
VIC. I like a De Soto better'n an old Pontiac.
WILMA. Pontiac's the best car there *is.* I wouldn't have an old De Soto.
BILLIE MAE. (*Spanking her doll.*) Be good, you bad baby!
WILMA. (*To Vic.*) Wanta play house?
VIC. How do ya play house?
WILMA. I'll be the mother. You be the father, and Billie Mae will be our baby girl.
VIC. What do we do?
WILMA. You just pretend to be grownups. It's fun. Come on and try.
VIC. It sounds stupid.
WILMA. Come on and play.
VIC. Nothin' else to do.
BILLIE MAE. My mother says I'm not supposed to play with boys.
WILMA. Your mother doesn't have to know, scaredy-cat!

BILLIE MAE. (*Looking at Vic.*) I don't like boys. Boys are rough.
WILMA. Oh, they are *not,* silly.
VIC. (*Coming into the barn.*) O.K., I'll give it a try. What do you want me to do?
WILMA. We just act like grownups. I know everything grownups do. I've watched my mother and daddy. I know everything they do.
VIC. Like what?
WILMA. You pretend like you're coming home from the office. You're real tired and I've got to get dinner.
VIC. What fun'll that be?
WILMA. (*Impatient with him.*) It's just the way you play the game.
VIC. O.K. (*Goes out and comes in again as a tired husband. He has no real gift for make-believe, but he tries to be convincing. He stretches his arms and flops into a chair.*) Sure had a busy day at the office today.
WILMA. Did you, Hubby dear? I played bridge with the Van Uppingtons! And afterward we took a ride in their Rolls Royce.
VIC. (*Himself.*) We supposed to be real rich?
WILMA. Sure.
VIC. (*Back into his role.*) I made fifty million dollars this afternoon. On the stock market.
WILMA. That's wonderful, dear. Now maybe I can get some new clothes. I'm so sick of all my old things.
VIC. I think maybe I'll get another new car. I think I could use a racing car, maybe.
WILMA. Would you like a cocktail, dear?
VIC. Sure.
WILMA. Baby's been very bad today, Hubby dear. I'm afraid you'll have to spank her.
VIC. All right.
WILMA. She just refused to do everything I told her to do, so you'll have to spank her to keep her from growing up to be a very bad girl.
VIC. All right. (*He picks up Billie Mae and starts to put her over his knee.*)
BILLIE MAE. (*Accusingly, to Wilma.*) I don't think this is fair.
WILMA. It's just *pretending,* Silly.

VIC. (*Spanking her lightly.*) You must be a good girl, Baby dear, and do everything your mother tells you.
WILMA. You must spank her hard, Hubby dear. She's been a very bad girl. (*Vic spanks her harder.*)
BILLIE MAE. (*Jumping off Vic's lap.*) I'm not going to play any more if you keep on spanking me.
WILMA. I guess she's been punished enough, Hubby dear. We'll let baby go back to bed now and go into the living room.
VIC. O.K.
BILLIE MAE. (*To herself.*) I don't see why I have to be the baby.
WILMA. (*To Vic.*) Would you like a cocktail, dear?
VIC. Sure.
WILMA. (*Herself, to Billie Mae.*) You be our maid now and bring us cocktails.
BILLIE MAE. I'm not going to play any more. You didn't tell me I'd have to be the maid.
WILMA. Just bring us a tray with something on it. Then you can go back to being Baby.
BILLIE MAE. I'm not having any fun at all. (*Sets a couple of dirty old glasses on a board and serves drinks.*) Here are your cocktails.
WILMA. Thank you, Maid. (*Billie Mae returns to the chest and sits there resuming the role of Baby. Wilma continues to Vic.*) I don't know what we're going to do with Maid, Hubby dear. She's just a terrible maid. She won't do anything I ask her.
VIC. Tell her we're going to fire her.
WILMA. But we can't fire her because help is so hard to get.
VIC. Why don't *you* do the work?
WILMA. Rich society women like me never do their own work. The Van Uppingtons have fifty maids, and butlers, too. And And chauffeurs. And . . . all kinds of servants. Do you like your cocktail, dear?
VIC. It's all right.
WILMA. Are you ready for dinner, dear?
VIC. I guess so.
WILMA. (*Calling.*) Maid! Maid! Hubby and I are ready for dinner now.
BILLIE MAE. (*In her own voice.*) You want me to be Maid again?
WILMA. Well, of course.

BILLIE MAE. (*In her role.*) Dinner is served.
WILMA. Say "Madam."
BILLIE MAE. Madam.
WILMA. That's better. (*To Vic.*) Will you take me to dinner, Hubby dear?
VIC. (*Getting up.*) O.K.
WILMA. We're having roast turkey and banana salad and angel-food cake à la mode.
VIC. Can't we have some sweet potatoes, too? I like sweet potatoes.
WILMA. All right, dear. We'll have sweet potatoes, too. (*They sit, one on either side of a barrel which serves as a table, and Billie Mae hands them imaginary dishes.*)
VIC. That's awful good turkey.
WILMA. It was the finest one I could buy. And isn't the banana salad good, too?
VIC. (*Pretending to eat.*) Sure. It's good, too.
WILMA. (*To Billie Mae.*) You can bring us the angel-food cake à la mode now.
BILLIE MAE. O.K.
WILMA. (*To Vic.*) I certainly hope you like the dessert, Hubby dear.
VIC. (*Himself.*) My mother just calls my father by his real name.
WILMA. I like to play the game the way *I'm* playing it.
VIC. It just sounds kind of crazy, callin' me "Hubby dear" all the time. No one does that.
WILMA. They do, too. (*Back in her role.*) Have you had enough dinner, Hubby dear?
VIC. I guess so.
WILMA. Shall we go into the living room and look at television?
VIC. I wanta go play poker.
WILMA. You can't leave me alone with Baby.
VIC. Oh, all right.
WILMA. I'll put baby to bed now. Will you come and kiss her good night?
VIC. Have I gotta kiss her?
WILMA. Well, sure, crazy! Are you afraid to kiss her?
VIC. No. I'm not afraid. It's just kinda crazy. That's all.
WILMA. (*To Billie Mae.*) Daddy and I have come to say good night, Baby dear!

BILLIE MAE. Good night!
WILMA. Say your prayers and sleep tight.
BILLIE MAE. O.K. (*Wilma kisses Billie Mae on the cheek, then turns to Vic.*)
WILMA. Now it's your turn. (*Vic leans over and kisses Billie Mae on the cheek.*)
VIC. Good night, Baby.
BILLIE MAE. Good night, Daddy.
WILMA. Shut your eyes real tight and go to sleep.
BILLIE MAE. O.K.
WILMA. *Real* tight.
BILLIE MAE. I've got 'em shut as tight as I can.
WILMA. I want Baby to grow up to be a very good girl, don't you, Hubby dear?
VIC. Yah . . . sure.
WILMA. I don't think I want to look at television, after all.
VIC. I don't care.
WILMA. I've had such a busy day, I'm awfully tired. I think I'll go to bed.
VIC. O.K.
WILMA. Are you ready to go to bed, too, Hubby dear?
VIC. Me? Oh . . .
WILMA. You've had such a busy day at the office. I think you should go to bed now and be sure to get your rest.
VIC. Well . . . I . . .
WILMA. Come on, Hubby dear.
VIC. (*He is not acting now.*) Well . . . what do we do?
WILMA. Our bedroom is in the hayloft. We'll go up there and leave Baby down here. (*She is completely self-possessed.*)
VIC. (*Clearing his throat.*) Uh . . . I don't think I wanta go to bed now. You go on to bed, and I . . . I'll go out for a walk.
WILMA. You can't. It's raining outside.
VIC. Oh!
WILMA. You're *scared.*
VIC. Who says so?
WILMA. It sure looks like it.
VIC. Well, I'm not, if you should happen to want to know.
WILMA. Well, come on then. It's just a game.
VIC. You mean . . . up there in the loft?
WILMA. Sure.

VIC. (*Completely at sea.*) Well . . . I'm not gonna play this game any more. This is a crazy game. I'm not playin'. (*He starts for his bike.*)
WILMA. I *told* you you're scared. (*Vic stops. He's not going to let himself be called scared.*) Boys are worse scaredy-cats than girls.
VIC. Well . . . gee whiz!
WILMA. And it's perfectly all right. There couldn't be anything wrong about it, cause we're just playing a game, aren't we? And we're doing everything our mothers and fathers do. So what could be wrong about it?
VIC. Well . . . I don't know, but . . .
WILMA. Unless you're just a plain old scaredy-cat.
VIC. I told you, I'm not scared.
WILMA. Then prove it!
VIC. You're sure crazy.
WILMA. *Prove* it!
VIC. Well . . . (*With a nod at Billie Mae, lying on the chest with her eyes shut.*) What about her?
WILMA. (*Whispering.*) She won't have to know anything.
VIC. Well . . . gee!
WILMA. Come on, scaredy-cat! (*She starts up the stairs to the loft.*)
VIC. Gee!
WILMA. If you don't follow me in two minutes, you're the biggest scaredy-cat that ever lived. So there! (*Continues up the stairs.*)
VIC. Shut up, will ya? I'm comin'.
WILMA. (*Stops and turns around.*) Then come along.
VIC. (*Following her, against his better judgment.*) I'm comin'. I'm comin'. (*He follows Wilma into the darkness of the loft, and there is a silence of several minutes. Then Billie Mae sits up and looks about her.*)
BILLIE MAE. What're you kids doin'? (*There is no response and she feels lonely and rejected.*) What's everyone doin'? (*Still no response. Billie Mae stands and walks around the barn, stopping at the foot of the stairs looking up.*) What're you crazy kids doin' up there in the loft? (*No response.*) I bet you're doin' something bad. (*No response.*) You kids are doin' something bad. (*No response. Billie Mae begins to sob.*) I don't like you any-

more, Wilma Wadsworth. I don't like you at all. (*Still no response.*) I'm going home now and tell my mother . . . (*No response.*) and I'll never come over to play with you again. (*Apparently Wilma is not concerned. Billie Mae moves to the door as though hoping someone will stop her.*) I'm going. (*No response.*) I'm going. (*No response. Now, the feeling of rejection is too strong for Billie Mae to hold. She bursts into sudden tears while she runs out of the barn.*) I'll never come back here to play with you again. I hate you, Wilma Wadsworth. I'll never be your playmate any more. I hate you. I hate you. (*The stage is empty now. There are several moments of absolute and mysterious silence.*)

CURTAIN

PROPERTY PLOT

On Stage

Nail kegs, barrels, tool chests
2 dolls
2 glasses

Off Stage

Bicycle (Vic)

THE MALL

CHARACTERS

MATRON 1

MATRON 2

CRONE 1

CRONE 2

BARNEY

DELL

GIRL

SAILOR

CLARA

MAN

This is a play that has come out of my own fantasies about characters I have noticed on summer strolls through Central Park, people who seem to live in the park during permissible weather, people who seem reduced to the pursuit of the most basic human needs. It was an attempt to write a play that made its dramatic point by a kind of combustion of forces rather than by a real narration. I had just wanted to contrast certain kinds of love and dramatize people in their pursuit of love. I found most interesting the older man's blind desperation in search for love in contrast with the young people's almost accidental discovery of love.

THE MALL

The scene is the mall of an amusement park in a seaside resort town. The promenade stretches across the stage, benches at the back, the sea presumably being the audience. The time is early fall, late September or early October, and the park is out of season. Summer is past and there is a feeling of rejection in the atmosphere. Behind the mall, in the distance, one can see the vast, deserted structure of the Playland. A Ferris wheel, a roller coaster, a parachute ride loom up in the background, great and useless structures waiting for their season to return. Closer behind the promenade are the banners heralding the freaks, likenesses of whom are pictured on the banners in fading primary colors, in almost grotesque caricature.

On one of the benches at the back of the promenade, facing the audience, sit two old crones, wine-heads, sharing a bottle of cheap wine from which they take occasional refreshing swallows. During the warm weather, they make the mall their home, bringing their wine there, sometimes sleeping there if they can avoid detection by the police. It is hard to imagine they have another home, if they do, for they and their garments are as weathered as the benches and the scenery surrounding them, all of which they seem a living part. They sit here through most of the day, observing the life around them, nudging each other and cackling together in mutual appreciation of the ironies they look for. On another bench sit two middle-aged matrons who have lingered for a short rest before returning to their respective homes after one of their daily walks, which they make together in the mutual hope of reducing. They have just sat down and are fanning themselves and getting their wind. The crones watch, with hawk eyes, their every movement, as though they sought in the faces and actions of humanity reassuring proof of life's futility, for the crones have de-

cided to let life pass them by, and they would never admit to a feeling of loss.

MATRON 1. Sort of a muggy day, isn't it?
MATRON 2. Yes. I don't like a muggy day, do you?
MATRON 1. No, I don't like muggy days at all. September's a sad month, don't you think? (*A pause.*) Or do you let yourself think about things like that?
MATRON 2. (*Musing.*) Now I don't know . . . if I've ever given the matter much thought. Let's see. Is September a sad month? Well, yes! Of course it is, isn't it? I mean, it's sad if you happen to like the summertime as much as Fred and I and the children do. Because in September, you know that summer's over and wintertime is ahead, and the weather will be cold. Yes . . . (*Looking around her.*) It's very sad.
MATRON 1. I think so. (*She's the type who is given to sudden changes of topic.*) Did you weigh yourself this morning?
MATRON 2. (*Nodding.*) I've lost *two* pounds.
MATRON 1. I wish *I* would.
MATRON 2. Oh, I'll probably put them right back on when I sit down to dinner tonight. I'm afraid the only way to lose weight is to go on a *severe* diet. I don't think these walks are doing either one of us any good.
MATRON 1. Well, I don't know about *you*, but I feel a hundred percent better.
MATRON 2. Oh, I feel better, too. It's so good for the circulation, but I don't think we're losing an ounce, either one of us. As a matter of fact, I think the walks are only making our flesh more solid. The only way to lose weight, I'm convinced now, is to go on a severe diet. Very severe.
MATRON 1. (*Sadly.*) Oh, dear! (*Her spirits back.*) Well, we've sat long enough, don't you think?
MATRON 2. Yes I do. (*Looks at watch.*) Besides, it's time I was getting home and fixing something for dinner. (*Up from their bench now, they start to make their way across stage, down the promenade. They notice the crones, drinking and cackling, and assume a somewhat superior attitude.*)
MATRON 1. Goodness, the people one sees here after sunset.
MATRON 2. It really isn't safe. Do you think we might trot?

MATRON 1. What?
MATRON 2. Maybe we'd lose more weight if we trotted . . . part of the time. I remember when I was a Girl Scout, we used to go on hikes, and we'd trot for fifty steps, then walk for fifty. That way, you don't get tired.
MATRON 1. Shall we try?
MATRON 2. I'm game. (*Standing side by side, they start off together, trotting, as though beginning a long relay race. The crones watch them off, cackling hilariously, as though they had just observed the prize absurdity of all time.*)
CRONE 1. Oh, God, Sister, wouldn't it kill ya?
CRONE 2. (*Who is given to mocking imitations.*) "I have to go home now and fix something for the children. Junior needs all his strength 'cause he's layin' the new maid, and little Geraldine is always hungry when she gets back from the opium den."
CRONE 1. Oh, God, Sister, ain't they a riot?
CRONE 2. Every day that passes, I thank the stars that whatever I be now, I ain't one of *them.*
CRONE 1. If they wanta lose weight, why don't they *quit* eatin', like we do, and live on the bottle? That'd take off a few pounds.
CRONE 2. And make 'em merrier company, too, wouldn't it, Sister?
CRONE 1. Sure, sure. (*Now a young sailor comes on, a good-looking fellow in his late teens. Apparently he is expecting to meet someone, and his face looks concerned. He glances at his watch and then leans on the balustrade at the back, preparing himself to wait. The crones notice him and nudge each other.*)
CRONE 2. (*Apropos of the sailor.*) Is it time for the lovers? Are the lovers comin' out?
CRONE 1. It's *always* time for the lovers, Sister. Love goes around the clock.
CRONE 2. Waitin' for his sweet patootie, ain't he?
CRONE 1. Sure, sure.
CRONE 2. Handsome lad, ain't he? Or is he your type?
CRONE 1. (*Slapping her thighs and laughing.*) Any type's my type, Sister. (*They laugh uproariously together.*)
CRONE 2. Every once in a while, I get to feelin' kinda spry even now, and I think of puttin' a few feathers in my hair and jewels on my fingers and goin' off somewhere to dance. Oh, God, Sister,

remember the days we used to dance. (*She gets to her feet and swings around in a waltz with an imaginary partner.*)

CRONE 1. You can still do it, Sister. Graceful as a swan.

CRONE 2. (*Returning to the bench, winded.*) Now I *can't,* Sister. Can't dance no more. I'm winded and weak already. Gimme the bottle. (*She takes a long, satisfying swallow.*)

CRONE 1. Well, you useda could. That's the important thing. You useda could.

CRONE 2. (*Holding her heart painfully.*) Oh, God, Sister, that liked to did me in. I just ain't what I used t'be. That's all. (*Barney and Dell come on. Both are men of around forty. Barney is a large man, Dell rather small. Barney wears no hat or necktie, and his suit, of a light washable material, is clean but unpressed. His shoes are scuffed and the frayed collar of his shirt is open at the neck. Dell wears the working clothes of a laborer. He is a slight man with large sad eyes. They are talking as they come on together.*)

BARNEY. (*Angrily impatient.*) Don't talk to me no more about it, Dell. I'm tellin' you to shut up.

DELL. Barney, I'm only tryin' to persuade you to take the doctor's advice.

BARNEY. Doctors or no doctors, I'm stayin' here till I find Clara.

DELL. Maybe Clara won't show up, Barney. It's been a long time and . . .

BARNEY. She'll be here. I know Clara.

DELL. (*Hopelessly.*) Oh, Barney. . . . (*When the two men sit together on a bench, crone 2 is quick to run to them with an outstretched hand.*)

CRONE 2. Help a poor widow woman, sirs. My house burned down last night and I got no money to take care of me and the kids. (*The men pay her no more attention than they do the breeze. She lingers for a moment. Something she detects in the men makes her suspicious and she runs back to crone 1.*) Oh, God, Sister, I didn't like the smell of them.

CRONE 1. What ya mean, Sister?

CRONE 2. I've smelled that smell before and I don't like it. It's that disinfectant they use in them loony bins. Before they let you out, they give you clothes that have soaked in it. Oh, God, Sister, it's a frightful smell to me. (*She is frightened.*)

CRONE 1. (*Passing the bottle.*) Console yourself, Sister. I ain't gonna let 'em take ya back. (*Crone 2 takes a long swallow of the wine.*)

DELL. Barney, the only thing for you to do is go out on that farm. You'd like it there, Barney. Things'd be quiet there and you could relax. There wouldn't be nothin' t'upset ya.

BARNEY. There ain't nothin' gonna upset me. I don't need to relax. I'm all right, I tell ya.

DELL. Barney, you *think* you're all right, but you're really not. You're still sick, Barney. The doctors said you was to keep quiet for a long time and not try to do much. They say if you get out and start chasin' gals again and start gettin' mad and excited and worked up again, you'll end up in the zoo again, in the same ward.

BARNEY. I been a long time in that zoo, and now I gotta have me a woman.

DELL. Clara's no *good* for you, Barney. You know she ain't.

BARNEY. Clara loved me once, Dell.

DELL. You don't understand women like Clara, Barney. They love *every*body once.

BARNEY. But Clara's gonna love me again.

DELL. How ya figure that?

BARNEY. 'Cause I got love streamin' outa my heart like heat from a furnace. And I can't let it go to waste. Someone has got to share it.

DELL. You're just buildin' yourself up to a big letdown, Barney. Lemme take you out to that farm, where it'd be peaceful and quiet.

BARNEY. (*With sudden ferocity.*) Mother Dell, I'm gonna call ya. You're worse'n a God damn woman with your advice and warnings and protections.

DELL. Now, Barney, take it easy. I'm not sayin' no more. It's just that I want you to be all right, Barney. *You* know that. It's just that I want ya to be all right.

BARNEY. (*Rising to full height.*) God damn ya, don't you know you can't make me all right, whatever's the matter with me? Don't you know that every man's gotta find his salvation somewhere inside hisself? And that regardless how sick I be, and how mixed up inside me, no amount of preachin', no amount of coaxin' and needlin' and cautionin' is gonna do any good unless I feel some change in *here.* (*He pounds his breast.*) That's where it's gotta come from.

DELL. I know, Barney.
BARNEY. And in *here* (*Indicating his heart.*) somethin' won't lemme rest, till I find Clara.
DELL. I'm sorry, Barney. I won't say no more.
BARNEY. All right, then. Let's sit peacefully and wait till she shows up.
DELL. All right, Barney. Anything you say. (*The two men sit, looking straight ahead, rather gloomily at the sea. Barney always wears an expression of trying to figure out some worrisome problem. Now a young girl, exceedingly pretty, comes on to meet the sailor.*)
GIRL. Have I kept you waiting long?
SAILOR. Not very, but it's seemed long.
GIRL. I got here as fast as I could. I had to lie to the folks to get out of the house. I told them I was going over to Helen's.
SAILOR. Gee . . . it's funny, isn't it?
GIRL. How d'ya mean?
SAILOR. I mean . . . when I came ashore this time, I didn't realize anything like this was gonna happen.
GIRL. I know what you mean.
SAILOR. 'Cause I never felt like this before . . . 'bout a girl. No fool!
GIRL. I never did either . . . about a *boy*.
SAILOR. Ernie and I left the boat together . . . he says have I got plans . . . I says no . . . so he tells me his girl Helen might be able to bring a friend . . . and I almost said, "Don't bother." Then I figured . . . why not? And I met you.
GIRL. And I almost didn't go when Helen called and asked me. 'Cause I met Ernie once before and didn't much like him. I just didn't s'pose he could have a friend . . . as nice as you.
SAILOR. Ernie's not a bad guy. Kinda loud but . . . (*On second thought.*) hey! You're the only girl ever told me I was nice.
GIRL. But you are.
SAILOR. No I ain't. Not really. It's just that . . . Well, when I'm with you, I *feel* nice . . . so then I'm nice. The rest of the time I'm pretty ornery . . . I think.
GIRL. No one's perfect.
SAILOR. No.
GIRL. Gee, I . . . I hate to go.

SAILOR. So do I. (*A pause.*) I got till midnight. Couldn't you stay with me till then?
GIRL. I just *can't*. I been out late the last three nights, and the folks are beginning to suspect something.
SAILOR. What the heck! You can do what you want to, can't you?
GIRL. I . . . I lied to you. I'm not twenty. I'm . . . seventeen.
SAILOR. Y'are? (*And as she nods.*) I'm nineteen. But I been on my own since I was a kid.
GIRL. I promised the folks I'd be right back. I don't want 'em to call Helen's and find out I'm not there.
SAILOR. Well . . . I guess this is it.
GIRL. I guess. Will you write?
SAILOR. I never *have* wrote letters . . . but I'll try.
GIRL. Just once in a while. Or just drop a post card that says *love*.
SAILOR. Okay.
GIRL. And . . . I'll remember you . . . as long as I live. I know.
SAILOR. (*With a feeling of futility.*) It just ain't fair. You go along your usual way, feelin' you're happy, takin' what comes, not carin' about too much one way or the other. . . . Then *zowie!* one day it happens. You fall in love. And it makes your whole life up until then seem kinda pointless. . . .
GIRL. That's the way *I* feel, too.
SAILOR. And then you can't just go back to your old life. 'Cause it don't seem no good.
GIRL. No. It don't.
SAILOR. (*Longingly.*) Can't you stay till my boat leaves?
GIRL. (*Frightened.*) I'll get an awful beating if I'm not back soon. My dad gets furious when I'm out late. I . . . I *gotta* go now. (*The sailor takes her in his arms and kisses her.*)
SAILOR. Goodbye!
GIRL. If you want me to, I'll not make any more dates till you come back.
SAILOR. I don't know . . . when I'll come back.
GIRL. (*Sobbing.*) I just can't bear to think I may never see you again.
SAILOR. Well . . . I'll probably be back in a year or so.
GIRL. A year! (*The girl runs off now, crying. The sailor stands a

few moments looking after her, then walks off sadly, in the other direction. The crones have watched the entire scene. They cackle quietly.)

DELL. (*To the crones.*) Can't you girls do anything but laugh?

CRONE 1. Might as well laugh as to cry, Mister.

CRONE 2. 'Cause if you ever get started crying, you'll never stop.

DELL. It don't sound very respectful. (*Crone 1 sees a familiar figure in the distance.*)

CRONE 1. (*Gloatingly.*) Here she comes, Miss La-De-Da!

CRONE 2. Dressed up in her Sunday best, out to find herself a *lovin'* man.

CRONE 1. She don't miss a night. That one! She can't go to sleep without her lovin' man. (*They both cackle gluttonously. Clara [Miss La-De-Da] comes strutting on, wearing a bright pink dress and shoes with high platform soles. Barney stands respectfully on seeing her approach.*)

DELL. Let *her* come to *you*, Barney. Take my advice. (*Barney remains silent and nervously alert. Clara's first preoccupation is with the crones.*)

CLARA. Why don't you old hags go off somewhere and die? (*The crones are invulnerable to any insult. They cackle.*) Why don't you old witches get on your brooms and ride off into the sky? (*The crones cackle louder.*) Old hags! Too old to have any fun yourselves. All you can do is sit here makin' fun of others. There oughta be a law against it. (*The crones continue to cackle.*) *I'll* never be like you. I'm still young. And I still got what it takes to make 'em take a second look. And I'm gonna have my fun. See? (*The crones cackle louder than ever. Angrily, Clara comes* c. *Barney now must speak out.*)

BARNEY. Clara!

CLARA. My God! Where'd *you* come from?

BARNEY. They let me go, Clara. First thing I do is come to see you.

CLARA. *When* did they let you go?

BARNEY. Just this morning.

CLARA. You sure you didn't sneak out or break out?

BARNEY. Cross my heart, Clara, and hope to die.

DELL. He's on the level, Clara. The doctors told 'im he's okay. He still has to take it easy for a while, but he's okay.

CLARA. What're you doin' here?

BARNEY. This is where we met, Clara. Remember? I come back to get you.
CLARA. I told you a hundred times, it's all over 'tween you and I.
BARNEY. (*With an almost childlike expression of hurt.*) You don't mean that, Clara.
DELL. Sure she does, Barney. C'mon, let's beat it. What d'ya say? (*Trying to divert him.*) I tell ya what, I know a place where there's hunnerds of good-lookin' women. Sure I do. Not so very far from here, either. What ya say we go?
BARNEY. (*Shoving Dell aside.*) Go way. (*Going to Clara.*) I come back to get *you*, Clara. I'm taking you with me.
CLARA. Says *you!*
BARNEY. I'm a new man, Clara. I got real love in my heart. I wanta share it.
CLARA. Listen to that talk!
BARNEY. I mean it, Clara. You gotta gimme a chance.
CLARA. You *had* your chance. It's all over now. Can't you get that through your thick skull? Now beat it.
BARNEY. I got real love in my heart, Clara. You don't know what it is. But it's a wonderful thing, *real* love. I know that now. There's nothin' in the world like it.
CLARA. Crap!
BARNEY. Real love, not just for a night or two, but for always, when two people live as *one*. Think of it, Clara. My life'd be yours. Your life'd be mine. Then we'd both have a bigger life, Clara, a life that'd mean somethin'.
CLARA. I never heard such crazy talk.
BARNEY. I know what real love is, Clara. I had it once, long time 'fore I met you. I had it. It was wonderful, Clara. My life was hers and her life was mine, and we had real happiness together.
CLARA. (*Exasperated.*) Oh, Lord! The same old line.
BARNEY. I gotta get that happiness back, Clara. Don't you understand?
CLARA. And can't *you* understand that I got enough happiness to suit *me?*
BARNEY. But you don't understand. I tell you what it's like. It's like you'd spent all your life livin' in one room, with the door closed, not knowin' that the door opened into another room, big-

ger, that looked out onto a beautiful view of the entire world. That's what *real* love is like, Clara.

CLARA. (*To Dell.*) Why don't ya take him back to the zoo?

DELL. C'mon, Barney old boy. You oughta know when you're not wanted.

BARNEY. (*Jerking himself free of Dell.*) God damn it, lemme be!

DELL. Take it easy, Barney.

BARNEY. I *been* in that other room, Clara. I know what real love is. I'd learn you.

CLARA. Now listen t'me. I come out here this evenin' 'cause I was expectin' to meet a very attractive gentleman that happened to speak to me th' other day as we was gettin' off the subway. He's due to show up any minute. Then we're goin' over to the Palace Ballroom and dance. I'd appreciate it if you was not around when he shows up.

BARNEY. Clara!

DELL. You heard what she said, Barney. C'mon!

BARNEY. (*Angrily insistent now, seizing Clara in his arms.*) God damn it, you're goin' *with* me. I got real love in my heart and I'm gonna learn ya what it is. You'll be happy after you know. We'll both be happy, Clara. Happier'n you ever thought you could be.

DELL. (*Turning his face, fearful of watching the scene.*) Barney . . . you mustn't do things like that.

CLARA. (*A tigress now, she kicks Barney in the groin and slaps at him viciously.*) Lay your hands off me, you maniac bum, or I'll call a cop and he'll take you back to the zoo where ya belong. I've heard enough of your love talk, and I ain't gonna listen to any more. I'm free, white and over twenty-one, and I don't have to put up with any more of this crap if I don't wanta. And I don't *wanta.* Can't you get that through your lunatic skull?

BARNEY. (*Fallen to the ground, cringing like a big, hearty dog that is punished for being too affectionate.*) Clara! Clara!

DELL. Clara, you shouldn't a done that. Barney's been sick.

CLARA. He's makin' *me* sick now.

BARNEY. (*Doubled up in pain.*) Clara, you was sweet to me once.

DELL. Fight back, Barney. Even if she *is* a woman. Fight back.

BARNEY. I can't, Dell.

DELL. You always was a great fighter. Makes me sick to see you like this.

BARNEY. I can't fight . . . a man in *love*, Dell, has got no fight. (*Barney remains squatting on the ground, Dell hovering over him protectively. The crones cackle with an appreciation of irony. The sailor and the girl now come on from opposite sides of the stage, walking very slowly, tentatively toward each other. There is an occasional sob and whimper from Barney. Clara walks restlessly about the mall, looking occasionally into the distance for her date.*)
SAILOR. (*Walking very slowly toward the girl.*) I . . . I just can't seem to go.
GIRL. (*Coming slowly toward the sailor.*) I can't either. (*They meet now, at* C., *and grasp each other passionately, then melt in a sustained kiss.*)
CRONE 1. (*Transfixed by the scene of the sailor and his girl.*) Oh, God, Sister, remember the days we had love?
CRONE 2. (*With a wistful countenance of momentary pain.*) Yes, Sister . . . I remember.
CLARA. (*Apparently sees her friend in the distance.*) It's about time. (*She waits at* R. *It is dusk now and the sky is beginning to darken.*)
SAILOR. (*With the girl in his arms.*) Maybe we could do something crazy . . . like gettin' married.
GIRL. Anything you say.
SAILOR. Just stay with me . . . as long as you can.
GIRL. I will.
SAILOR. What'll you do about your old man?
GIRL. I don't know.
SAILOR. Will he beat you?
GIRL. Prob'ly.
SAILOR. Cri-miney!
GIRL. It's all right. I don't care. (*They sit together in a fast embrace. The two crones gaze on them as though they were figures in a dream.*)
CRONE 1. You're cryin', Sister.
CRONE 2. Am I?
CRONE 1. I am, too. We gotta stop. (*Barney still remains on the ground, nursing his wounds. Dell still is with him. Now Clara's boy friend comes on, a man close to forty, good-looking, sharply dressed. Clara becomes very seductive, a sly insinuation in her voice.*)

CLARA. Well . . . good evening!
MAN. Same to you.
CLARA. Are you the man who said you'd take me to the Palace Ballroom?
MAN. I'm the man.
CLARA. Well . . . I'm waitin'.
MAN. . . . Unless . . . you had some other place in mind, perhaps. Some place . . . more private.
CLARA. I do . . . but we'll have time for that later.
MAN. 'Cause when I look at *you*, Baby, I got other things on my mind than dancin'.
CLARA. (*Laughing coarsely.*) How many girls you said that to?
MAN. Hell, I don't know. But every time I say it, I *mean* it, Baby.
CLARA. C'mon, Daddy. Let's paint that ballroom red. (*They strut off together arm in arm, the crones, of course, watching and cackling. It is night now. Barney staggers to his feet to watch them after they have disappeared. Then he calls out in a shattering voice.*)
BARNEY. Whore! Bitch! That's all y'are, a two-bit whore! A two-timin' bitch!
DELL. Take it easy, Barney. There's cops around.
BARNEY. (*Falling to the ground, pounding it with his fists, sobbing hysterically.*) Oh, God! And sweet, sweet Jesus! Where is there someone who can take my love? Where is there someone who can bear it?
DELL. (*Sympathetically.*) I told ya that's what'd happen, Barney. (*Barney bawls like a wounded stag, as Dell kneels by his side attentively. The two crones cackle from their perch in the background. The sailor and his girl sit on a bench in a fast embrace. The two matrons return, trotting together. They stop for a moment to get their wind, and take notice of the characters around them.*)
MATRON 1. (*Apprehensive.*) Oh, goodness! Let's not stay here.
MATRON 2. No. This is no place for us. (*They trot off together.*)

CURTAIN

PROPERTY PLOT

On Stage

Several park benches

Personal

Bottle of wine (Crones)
Watches (Matrons, and Sailor)

AN INCIDENT AT THE STANDISH ARMS

CHARACTERS

WOMAN

MAN

GIRL

AN INCIDENT AT THE STANDISH ARMS

The scene is the rather pretentiously stylish living room of a luxurious apartment in a large American city. When the curtain rises the stage is empty. Suddenly, a woman comes running into the room as though fleeing someone. She is quite an attractive woman in her mid-thirties, dressed now in a filmy negligee, her bare feet in satin sandals, her long, wavy hair loose. There is a desperation about her now, as though she hoped to find a secret panel somewhere in the walls that would suddenly open and provide a means for her disappearance. But she can only clutch at the air blindly and stifle the compulsory screams in her throat. There being no magic exit, she finally runs to a corner of the room like a guilty child seeking her own punishment. She stands there waiting breathlessly for the man to appear. After a few moments, he appears, coming from the same room from which the woman came, presumably a bedroom. He is a big dark man of rough good looks, maybe an Italian. He is a taxicab driver, and he looks now for the cap which he left in the living room before entering the bedroom. When he comes out, he is buttoning his shirt. He looks at the woman amused and mystified.

MAN. Lady, fer Chris' sakes, whatsa matter? (*The woman trembles in her corner but she cannot answer.*) I ask ya, whatsa matter, lady? Ya got sick?

WOMAN. (*Refusing to look at him, gasping her words.*) Go! Please go!

MAN. Oh, so that's it. Ya wanta get rid of me now, don't ya? Is that it?

WOMAN. Please . . . I don't wish to seem rude . . . but I . . . I really must ask you to go now.

MAN. Whatsa matter? Don't I look so good to ya now that it's all over?

WOMAN. Please try to understand. I don't wish to seem rude. I wouldn't be rude to you for anything in the world. But I . . . I must be alone now.
MAN. Whatsa matter? Is Papa on his way home? That it? You're scared Papa's gonna come home and find me here?
WOMAN. (*Imploringly.*) Please! Please!
MAN. Look, lady, what's so terrible if someone does find me here? I brought you home in a cab, din I? Maybe I helped you carry your packages up here to your apartment.
WOMAN. I . . . I have a young daughter. She'll be coming home from school any minute now.
MAN. What do you think I'm gonna do, stay here and make faces at her?
WOMAN. The . . . the management of the Standish Arms . . . they're very observing . . . I . . . I would be terribly embarrassed if they . . . if they suspected anything.
MAN. Look, lady, I got a family, too. I got three kids. Yah. I don't want trouble no worse'n you do. You ever stop to think a that?
WOMAN. I . . . I haven't a husband any more . . . I . . . I'm divorced.
MAN. Sure. I figured that. Look, lady, you could spare me just one little drink before I go, couldn't ya?
WOMAN. (*Pointing.*) There's the bar. You can help yourself. I . . . I'll have one, too. (*The man pours two drinks. She downs hers in one gulp. He is more relaxed.*)
MAN. Jesus, I never saw such a change in anyone. You got in my cab down town, and I thought "Gee, here's a real doll. I could go for a littla that." Then, I could see ya lookin' at me from the back seat. Yah, I could see you were kinda goin' for me, too.
WOMAN. I . . . I only thought you looked like someone I . . . once knew.
MAN. Anyway, you liked what you was lookin' at, baby. Don't deny it.
WOMAN. I . . . I don't deny it. I . . . I did notice you.
MAN. Look, baby, this happens to me a lot. Yah. Sometimes I get a broad that wants to pay for her ride that way. I say, nothin' doin'. You'd be surprised, lady, some of the homes I been invited

into, in this town. Plenty a places, just as knocked out as the Standish Arms.

WOMAN. I . . . I'm really not interested.

MAN. But I never saw a dame *turn* like you do. You ask me to come up to your apartment, and you throw your arms around me when we get here and start givin' me the works . . .

WOMAN. (*Hiding her face.*) Please!

MAN. And then it's all over and ya can't wait for me to get out. Ya can't even look me in the face. What kind of a dame are you?

WOMAN. I . . . I really shouldn't have . . . asked you up. It was wrong of me. I . . . I don't know what made me do it.

MAN. Well, *I* know what made you do it, lady, and if you don't, you better get wise to yourself. You're a sexy broad.

WOMAN. Please! Don't say that.

MAN. Most girls'd think I was givin' 'em a compliment.

WOMAN. It's just that I get very lonely at times, since I was divorced, and I . . . I miss my husband in these ways, and . . .

MAN. Lady, I understand. You don't have to tell me a thing. I'm only too glad to oblige.

WOMAN. No. It isn't right. It isn't right.

MAN. Well . . . I don't argue with myself about things like that.

WOMAN. Please! When you go down, would you take the service elevator? And go out the back way? If the elevator man and the doorman see you, they'll become suspicious.

MAN. Oh, for Christ sake!

WOMAN. I hate to ask it of you, but surely you understand.

MAN. Yah. I understand. (*There is a pause.*) Look, lady. This whole thing was your idea to begin with, and I'm not makin' any complaint even now, but . . . I hate to leave a woman like this, feelin' like I'd done dirty on her somehow. Couldn't ya give me a li'l hug now? How 'bout it, huh? (*He places an appealing hand on her shoulder.*) C'mon, let's have a li'l kiss before I go, shall we? Just to show we can be friends. I ain't gonna pester ya, fer Christ sake. I'll probably never see you again. But . . . let's leave off friendly. How's about it?

WOMAN. (*Shrinking.*) Not now. I . . . I couldn't.

MAN. (*Now anger and insult seize him.*) Then God damn you and your hypocrite ways! To hell with you and all your kind.

(*He seizes a costly Chinese vase from a table and flings it to the floor.*) You've made me feel cheap, God damn you! You've made me feel cheap! (*He jerks his cap onto his head and bolts out of the door, slamming it behind him. The woman shrieks and falls to the floor.*)
WOMAN. My God, what have you done? What did you do that for? How can I ever explain? (*With hurried anxiety, she picks up the pieces of the vase and dumps them into a waste-basket. Then she falls onto the divan, shaking with tears and humiliation, crying out in a sort of frantic prayer.*) Oh, God, what makes me do these things? Dear God, what makes me do them? (*She lies prostrate on the divan, shaking and sobbing. In several minutes, her young daughter, aged twelve, enters, and the woman sits up, drying her eyes, assuming her normal respectable posture.*)
GIRL. I'm home, Mama. I'm home.
WOMAN. (*Embracing the girl.*) Hello, dear!
GIRL. (*In an indignant voice.*) Mother, I want you to write a note to my teacher and ask her please to change my seat, because there's a perfectly horrid girl who sits across from me. She uses all sorts of filthy words, and she stinks because she never bathes, and she wears ugly, dirty dresses. I refuse to go to school if I have to sit next to anyone like her. Promise me you'll write the note to my teacher, Mother. Promise me.
WOMAN. Yes, dear. I promise.

CURTAIN

PROPERTY PLOT

On Stage

Stylish living room furniture:
  Divan, chairs, tables, lamps, etc.
Bar, with bottles and glasses
Table, with Chinese vase
Wastebasket
Taxi driver's cap

THE STRAINS OF TRIUMPH

CHARACTERS

ANN

TOM

OLD MAN

BEN

1ST ATHLETE

2ND ATHLETE

Success is counted sweetest
By those who ne'er succeed.
To comprehend a nectar
Require sorest need.

Not one of all the purple host
Who took the flag today
Can tell the definition,
So clear, of victory,

As he, defeated, dying,
On whose forbidden ear
The distant strains of triumph
Break, agonized and clear.

EMILY DICKINSON

THE STRAINS OF TRIUMPH

The scene is laid at the side of a small hillock behind which lies an open field. In the far background are bright-colored pennants flying in the breeze, and we hear the distant sound of strident band music, proclaiming victory. Mixed with the music is the sound of cheering voices.

VOICES. Give 'em the axe, the axe, the axe!
Give 'em the axe, the axe, the axe!
Yeh for Simpson!
Simpson won the fifty-yard dash!
Next event!
Ready for the next event!
Give 'em the axe, the axe, the axe!
Give 'em the axe, the axe, the axe!
(*An old man, bent over his cane, comes walking onto the scene, drawn by the music and voices. He goes to the top of the hillock and stands, his back to the audience, watching the games in the distance. Now a young girl, Ann, comes running, laughing onto the scene. She is about nineteen, pretty, dressed simply in sweater and skirt, her hair free. Following fast behind her is Tom, a young athlete, dressed in the gray sweat suit and track shoes provided by his college. He catches up with Ann, grabs her in his arms and kisses her. Then they laugh lovingly together. Ann suddenly notices the old man, who thus far has not turned to watch the young people but still stands, his back to the audience, looking off into the distance.*)
ANN. He'll see.
TOM. What if he does? (*Thoughtless but not cruel.*) He's just an old man.
ANN. Still, he can see us.
TOM. What if he does see me? What if he does? (*He grabs her in his arms and kisses her again. Then he proclaims loudly, attracting the old man's attention.*) Look, everybody! I'm kissing Ann. Ann and I are in love. I'm kissing her. See? (*Ann in his arms, he looks closely into her eyes.*) Now, I've told the whole world, and the

whole world may be watching. Does that keep me from kissing you?
ANN. Tom, Ben will be coming along any minute, and I don't want Ben to know.
TOM. (*Recklessly.*) To hell with Ben!
ANN. But I *like* Ben.
TOM. You *like* Ben, but you're in *love* with me. Admit it.
ANN. I do admit it, Tom.
TOM. Then forget about Ben. That's the only thing you can do. Forget him.
ANN. I don't want to hurt his feelings.
TOM. But you've *got* to hurt his feelings.
ANN. I mustn't. Ben and I grew up together. I know how deeply he feels things, much more than he shows.
TOM. I've had *my* feelings hurt, fer crying out loud! Before I came to college, I was nuts about a girl in high school, and she gave me the air. Yah! For a long time after that, I couldn't eat, I couldn't study, I didn't wanta see anyone. But I got over it. I learned to take it. It's just part of growing up.
ANN. I know. The same thing happened to me in high school. I was awfully fond of a boy and he started dating my best friend. I cried and cried and cried. I sulked around the house until Mother took me to see a doctor. Do you know what he did? He gave me vitamin shots. Honestly! (*They laugh.*)
TOM. But you got over it, didn't you?
ANN. (*Their mood is still jovial. Their present love is too much with them for the past to cast a gloom.*) Yes, I got over it.
TOM. And that's what Ben has got to do. Get over it. Even if he *is* my buddy, I gotta admit, he's spoiled. He's gotta learn to take his medicine like everyone else.
ANN. (*Troubledly.*) I think he's suspected something already.
TOM. After the races, we'll tell him.
ANN. Both of us?
TOM. Why not? We'll go to him together and say, "Ben, Ann and I are in love. She's going to wear my fraternity pin. Sorry, old man. These things are tough, but human beings always get over 'em. It's just part of growing up."
ANN. I dread telling him. But I'll feel better about it if we're together.

TOM. Just think, Ann. We'll always be together *now.* (*He takes her in his arms.*)
ANN. (*Truly in love.*) Oh, Tom! (*He kisses her.*)
TOM. We're as one person already. Aren't we?
ANN. Yes, Tom. I feel it, too.
TOM. It's a magical process, *love,* isn't it? One day, two people are separate individuals, each going his own way; on another day, they meet and fall in love, and they become like one. Without you now, I'd feel just half a man.
ANN. I feel the same, but I never realized, before we met, that I was incomplete in any way.
TOM. (*Taking her in his arms again.*) Oh, Ann!
ANN. Tom! (*He kisses her again, while the voices and music come up from the background. The old man watches, his back still to the audience. He jumps up and down with enthusiasm.*)
VOICES. Yea! Yea! (*In a chant.*) V-I-C-T-O-R-Y!
That's the way to spell it!
Here's the way to yell it! (*A bombastic shout.*)
VICTORY!
Yeh! Yeh! Pin a medal on Cutler! Cutler won the hurdles. Yeh! Yeh!
TOM. (*Releasing Ann.*) Did you hear that? Cutler won the hurdles. This is a big day for us. We better go back.
ANN. Can't we sit together until your event?
TOM. *Some*how. We'll manage somehow. (*They run off together arm in arm. Slowly Ben comes on from behind the hillock, where he stands for a few moments, watching Ann and Tom disappear. One must get the feeling that he has been watching them and knows in his heart what has happened. First there is a look of intense anguish on his face, and he stands rigid with bitterness and rage. Then gradually the intensity subsides, and his features and his body relax into sad resignation, and he lopes down the hillock, getting to the bottom, letting himself fall to the ground, lying sprawled there. Slowly, the old man takes cognizance of him and, still standing at the top of the hillock, speaks.*)
OLD MAN. (*In the gentlest voice.*) Have you been hurt?
BEN. (*Lifting his head.*) I'm all right.
OLD MAN. Is there anything the matter?
BEN. (*A pause elapses while he considers the question and decides to avoid answering. Instead he asks directly:*) Who are you?

OLD MAN. I recently heard myself referred to as "just an old man." That's true, of course, but my students refer to me as Professor Benoit, Associate in the Department of Ancient Languages.

BEN. I apologize for not recognizing you, Professor.

OLD MAN. No one ever recognizes a professor. Don't apologize. (*There is a long pause. Ben is trying to hold back tears. The old man, perhaps sensing Ben's despair, tries to sound diverting.*) There's such a crowd there, isn't there? I honestly believe I never saw so many people. Wouldn't the Board of Regents be pleased if my classes started filling up that way? (*Suddenly Ben bursts out in uncontrollable tears. The old man is very concerned, hurrying down to Ben's side.*) My boy! My boy!

BEN. (*Fighting off the old man's almost motherly protection.*) Go away, old man. Go away!

OLD MAN. (*He seems to understand and withdraws, going back to the top of the knoll.*) Very well. I'm sorry I interfered. I shall mind my business and continue watching the games. (*Now he stands as he did before, his back to Ben, who lies face down on the ground, all but writhing with the pain of his rejection. Background voices and music come up again. The band, with "Boola Boola," and the cheering squad start off in unison, the voices sounding vindictive.*)

VOICES. Give 'em the axe, the axe, the axe!
Give 'em the axe, the axe, the axe!
Give 'em the axe!
Give 'em the axe!
Give 'em the axe! Where?
Right in the neck, the neck, the neck!
Right in the neck, the neck, the neck!
Right in the neck!
Right in the neck!
Right in the neck there!

(*Now the voices seem to explode into a vocal shower of calls, whistles and shrieks.*)

OLD MAN. (*His back to the audience, speaking to himself and anyone who cares to listen.*) I look forward to the games all year long. Last October I bought my season ticket to the Student Activity Program and have attended all the events during the year. I happened upon the little knoll a few years ago when I was out on one of my walks, and I saw what a splendid view it offers of the stadium, so I've been coming here, where I enjoy being a solitary spectator. You see, I'm rather a childish old man, and I get so excited watching the games that I'm embarrassed for others to see me, particularly my students, who surely would think I had taken leave of my senses if they saw me jumping up and down and pounding the air with my fists. (*He gives a little chuckle.*) So I gave my ticket to the cleaning woman. And it pleased me to do that, for I can't afford to pay her much and she loves the games, too. *Every*one loves the games. Although not everyone cares to contend in them. I never did care to. I was studious even as a child. And I was frail. I was always getting a nosebleed. So I made myself content to watch and not participate. I suppose all people are divided into two groups, those who participate and those who watch and observe. Sometimes, in my more melancholy moments, I wonder if I have lived life at all, if my life has not been, rather, a period of observation on earth, watching others live, studying the way they live and commenting on their success or failure in the process. Being very moved by them at times, but still detached so that my envy of their success is fleeting, and my sadness at their failure passes when I sit down at a good meal or take a glass of sherry. *Once* I was in love, and it terrified me. She was so beautiful, so tender, so fine that I trembled in her mere proximity. The reality of her seemed too much for me to bear, and I fled. I could not accept the responsibility of loving her. (*He sighs.*) Alas! sometimes I am very lonely, of course. I go to bed, some nights, despondent, but I always awake feeling free. But I must admit, I always hurry to my office to become involved in my research as quickly as possible, for if I remain idle very long, I sometimes become very depressed. (*A rousing cheer comes from the stadium.*)

VOICES. V-I-C-T-O-R-Y!
That's the way to spell it.
Here's the way to yell it!
VICTORY!
Yeh! Yeh!
Hopkins won the discus!
Yeh, Hopkins!
He's our boy! Yeh, Hopkins!

OLD MAN. They're putting Ronnie Hopkins up on their shoulders now, carrying him through the stadium. I had the lad in class last year. I found him at times almost belligerent about learning, or about not learning. "What do I care about ancient history?" he used to bellow. "Why should I spend my time worrying about what happened in the past? *I'm* living *now.*" "True," I always replied to him, "but sometimes the present means more to us if we see it in terms of what has been before." He would shake his head then and mumble some incoherent protest. After grave consideration, I finally passed him in the course but with a very low grade. He never even learned to spell *Nebuchadnezzar.*

VOICES. Yeh, Hopkins!

He's our boy!

Trot him round the field again!

OLD MAN. (*Turns his back on the scene in the stadium and looks down at Ben, who still lies sprawled at the foot of the hillock, his face in his hands.*) Where do you come from, young man?

BEN. (*Lifting his face, wiping away a few tears with the back of his hand.*) A little town . . . in Iowa.

OLD MAN. I was through Iowa once on a train.

BEN. I wish to God I was back there.

OLD MAN. It never does any good to go back. Our memory always idealizes the past. If we return to it, we never find there what we're seeking.

BEN. Maybe.

OLD MAN. What are you studying here at the University?

BEN. I . . . I hope to become an architect.

OLD MAN. And you're an athlete, too? Remarkable.

BEN. I'm supposed to run in the relays.

OLD MAN. But aren't you going to?

BEN. I . . . I don't think so.

OLD MAN. But they'll be waiting for you at the stadium.

BEN. Let them.

OLD MAN. They're counting on you.

BEN. What if they are!

OLD MAN. I should think you'd be eager to start your race.

BEN. I was . . . until a few minutes ago.

OLD MAN. And now?

BEN. (*Slowly, with bitter distaste.*) Races suddenly seem . . . hateful and terrifying.

OLD MAN. Why?
BEN. I never knew before . . . what it is to lose. (*Another shout of victory goes up.*)
VOICES. Yeh, Pomeroy!
Give 'em the axe, the axe, the axe!
Give 'em the axe, the axe, the axe!
Yeh! Yeh!
OLD MAN. (*Still in thought, responding to Ben.*) Yes, it's terrifying—to lose. (*Two young athletes, Ben's age, run on together.*)
1ST ATHLETE. Hey, Ben, we been lookin' all over for you.
2ND ATHLETE. You're in the next event. Get goin'.
OLD MAN. (*Gently urging him.*) Go on, young man.
BEN. (*To the other athletes.*) Why should I?
1ST ATHLETE. What?
2ND ATHLETE. For crying out loud, Ben, you can't let us down.
BEN. I'm not going to run in the race.
1ST ATHLETE. Well . . . I'll be a . . .
2ND ATHLETE. Have you gone nuts?
OLD MAN. Young man, think carefully about this. Try to persuade yourself . . .
BEN. I've made up my mind. (*There is a long pause.*)
1ST ATHLETE. What'll we tell the coach, Ben?
BEN. Whatever you like.
2ND ATHLETE. Who'll he put in your place?
BEN. He'll find someone.
1ST ATHLETE. (*Angrily.*) You're a lousy sport.
2ND ATHLETE. I agree.
BEN. I suppose I am.
1ST ATHLETE. (*With a look at 2nd athlete.*) Well . . . let's go back and give 'em the news.
2ND ATHLETE. O.K. (*The two athletes run off together. Ben stands rigid. The old man watches with keen and sympathetic interest. The cheering and the music resume in the background.*)
OLD MAN. (*Finally.*) It shouldn't frighten you so . . . to lose.
BEN. No . . . it *shouldn't.* (*Tom and Ann come running on together. Ann calls.*)
ANN. Ben! (*Ben turns as if trying to escape them.*)
TOM. Ben, we have to talk to you. (*Ben waits. They come to his side.*)

ANN. You knew? I'm wearing Tom's pin? (*Ben nods.*) I wanted to be the one to tell you, Ben.
TOM. We were *both* gonna tell you, Ben.
ANN. Ben . . . (*Ben stands attentive but keeps his eyes off both of them.*) I just wanted to tell you . . . I really like you an awful lot.
TOM. Ann still thinks the world of you, Ben . . . and I guess you know how I feel, don't you? I feel, we'll always be buddies. (*He puts an arm around Ben's shoulder.*)
ANN. Tom says you're the best friend he ever had.
TOM. And I mean it.
ANN. I don't see any reason why we can't still be friends, Ben. Maybe better friends than before.
TOM. Ben—why don't you come to the Varsity with us tonight? If you don't have a date, you can dance with Ann all you want to . . .
ANN. I'd love it, Ben.
TOM. Come on, Ben. You'll get over this eventually. Why not now?
BEN. (*Words come with difficulty.*) I hadn't planned . . . to go to the Varsity.
VOICES. (*Calling from the stadium.*) Tom! Hey, Tom! Where are you, Tom? Your event is next, Tom!
TOM. Golly, I'm next. I gotta beat it. Wait for me at the gate, Ann. (*Tom starts, but Ben holds him.*)
BEN. (*Grasping Tom's sleeve.*) Tom! (*He is trembling with rage.*)
TOM. Hey, Ben, I gotta go.
BEN. (*Sobbing in rage.*) Damn you, Tom! Damn you! (*He seizes Tom by the throat.*)
TOM. (*Freeing himself from Ben's hold.*) Ben!
ANN. Ben, you can't hate Tom.
TOM. (*Going to Ben.*) I don't want you to hate me, Ben.
BEN. (*Realizing the futility of his gesture.*) Go on.
TOM. I don't want you to hate me, Ben.
BEN. Go on. They're waiting. (*Tom runs off.*)
ANN. You mustn't blame Tom for what happened, Ben. It's my fault as much as his. We've fallen in love. Don't you see? It wasn't something that we did intentionally. It . . . just happened.
BEN. I don't feel much like talking, Ann.

ANN. I understand. Please try to look on us as friends, Ben. Please.
BEN. I'm not sure I know how to look on anyone any more, Ann.
ANN. Just remember that we do like you. We do.
BEN. "Like?"
ANN. You'll find another girl in time, Ben. A girl who'll love you just as much as I love Tom.
BEN. Some people . . . don't find love . . . very easily, Ann.
ANN. In another few weeks you'll wonder what you ever saw in me.
BEN. Are you going to be married?
ANN. This summer. Oh, Ben, we want you as best man, and we want you as our friend forever. (*Kisses him on the cheek.*) Goodbye, Ben. (*She runs off. Ben slips to the ground, his body convulsed with growing sobs, writhing in mortal agony. The old man, who has stood withdrawn on his hillock through all this scene, now makes a tentative gesture, as though hoping to console Ben, but then decides it might be better not to interfere, and so returns his attention to the field below where trumpets are sounding for a new event and the band plays "Boola Boola." But he cannot help recalling Ben's prostrate body on the ground, and so he turns again from the games and goes to him, speaking softly.*)
OLD MAN. Young man . . . (*Ben does not move.*) you mustn't let yourself feel so deeply.
BEN. Now I know why people go mad and kill.
OLD MAN. Yes. Some people go mad and kill.
BEN. (*In a fury of protest.*) I don't *want* to hate. I don't *want* to.
OLD MAN. No one wants to.
BEN. (*Jumps to his feet, runs to the right, calling into the distance.*) Tom, come back! I won't hate you, Tom. I won't hate you. (*Down in the stadium, a gun is fired starting the race.*)
OLD MAN. He won't hear you now. He's in the race.
BEN. (*In a weak voice, returning.*) Tom!
OLD MAN. Young man, maybe you'd like to come up on my hillock and watch.
BEN. No.
OLD MAN. Oh, the games are most exciting. Come and watch. Here beside me.

BEN. I've always played in the games. I feel humiliated just to stand and watch.
OLD MAN. Oh, come now. One doesn't have to run in the races to enjoy them. Sometimes I think I enjoy the relays more than anyone, standing up here on my lonely hillside. And I can spell *Nebuchadnezzar*, too. (*He chuckles. Ben is still reluctant.*) Come along. (*Ben slowly rises and starts up the hillside, as though trying an unheard of experiment. The old man displays the view as though it were a great painting.*) Up here, you can see them all, and the view gives them perspective. Isn't it a magnificent sight? (*Ben looks intently into the distance.*) And when the games are over, you don't have to fight your way through all the crowd.
BEN. (*With passive interest.*) Look! Tom won his race, didn't he?
OLD MAN. Yes. He won. He won. And now they're starting a new event. Oh, listen to the trumpets and the bumptious band. And see the cheer leaders jumping up and down. (*We hear these sounds.*)
BEN. Yes, it all looks very different, from a distance.
OLD MAN. It's beautiful, isn't it? And exciting?
BEN. Yes. From here, it's beautiful and exciting. (*The band plays "Boola Boola" as the two men stare down in the distance.*)

CURTAIN

PROPERTY PLOT

Personal

Cane (Old Man)